PETER
THE LORD'S CAT
AND OTHER UNEXPECTED
OBITUARIES FROM
WISDEN

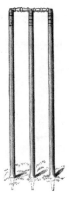

PETER
THE LORD'S CAT
AND OTHER UNEXPECTED
OBITUARIES FROM

WISDEN

EDITED BY

Gideon Haigh

Aurum

First published 2006 by Aurum Press Ltd
25 Bedford Avenue
London WC1B 3AT
www.aurumpress.co.uk

by arrangement with John Wisden & Co.

The obituaries collected in this book were first published in
Wisden Cricketers' Almanack.

Wisden and its woodcut device are registered trademarks of
John Wisden & Co Ltd.

A catalogue record for this book is available from the British Library.

ISBN-10 1 84513 163 0
ISBN-13 978 1 84513 163 0

1 3 5 7 9 10 8 6 4 2
2006 2008 2010 2009 2007

Designed by Peter Ward
Typeset in Adobe Jenson by M Rules
Printed and bound in Great Britain by MPG Books, Bodmin, Cornwall

INTRODUCTION

It has been said that, not being an especially religious people, the English devised cricket as a vision of the eternal. The game's vocabulary certainly provides regular intimations of mortality. A 'dead bat' is a useful accessory; a 'dead ball' is provided for in the laws; 'dead Tests' are not unknown. Batsmen can enjoy 'lives', but learn to dread the 'lethal' delivery; that is, when they have not first 'self destructed' after a 'rush of blood'. To be captured plumb lbw is to be 'dead in front'; to be bowled is to hear the 'death rattle'. To bat as a match or innings concludes is to be 'in at the death'; to bowl at the same time is to be delegated 'the death overs'. Then the 'post mortems' begin.

Death of the permanent rather than the passing kind, furthermore, has long been a salient feature of *Wisden Cricketers' Almanack*. Since inaugurating the custom in 1892, cricket's biggest and yellowest book has published more than 10,000 obituaries, covering the great, the good, the conventional, the heterodox, the remembered and the forgotten. Over time, in fact, *Wisden*'s annual chronicle of death notices has acquired quasi-institutional status, its glimpses of the love of cricket in all its varied forms somehow a source of vitality and regeneration.

Forty years ago, in one of the loveliest of cricket essays, Ronald Mason cherished a Cheshire nurseryman called Frederick Hyland, an 'inconspicuous embodiment of obscurity' who had attracted the attention of cricket's recording angel by spending two overs on a first-class cricket field representing Hampshire in a rain-ruined game: 'He retired, after the fashion of all good philosophers, to cultivate his garden; but by his ten wet minutes on the first-class field he had as irrevocably joined the ranks as W.G. had, whose playing life in that region spanned 44 years. In the sight of the eternities in and beyond history, 44 years and ten minutes are as one: Frederick J. Hyland, cricketer and nurseryman, may, in the sight of all us envious idealists beyond the pale, stand kin to Grace in honour. Of his kind is the game given its enduring strength and fascination.'

Hyland is one of the 250 or so obituaries in this volume. His kind is its subject: men who squeezed cricket into their lives rather than their lives into cricket. Some of them are men who achieved high office: five kings, one British prime minister, two Australian prime ministers, governors of Canada, Australia and the Windward Islands, two Lords Chief Justice, ministers of defence and labour, a Field Marshal, a president of the Board of Education, a director of the Bank of England and a member of the International Olympic Committee. But mostly it attests the breadth of cricket's appeal.

Here to be found are not merely president of the Football Association, president of the Institution of Mechanical Engineers, secretary-general of the International Planned Parenthood Federation, US cultural attaché to Italy, Chief Psychologist at the Directorate for the Selection of Personnel at the War Office, chief of staff for the UN peace-keeping force in Cyprus, chairman of selectors for the British equestrian team, head porter of Trinity College, Indian ambassador to Paris, and honorary weedkiller at Lord's, but also a music-hall artiste, a monk, a missionary, the father of the English bar, the father of English socialism, a distinguished art critic, a learned Arabist, an expert on Roman pottery, a self-made textile magnate, a long-distance driver, a designer of missile nosecones, a biographer of de Gaulle, a producer of *ITMA* and a star of *Doctor Who*. Then there are the

frankly unclassifiable, such as Gwynfor Evans, whose threat of a hunger strike was instrumental in expediting a Welsh-language television station, and Kenneth Gandar-Dower, who represented Cambridge at six sports, flew a private plane to India, became a noted big-game shot and introduced a team of Kenyan cheetahs to London where they set speed records on its greyhound tracks – this in a life ended by war at 36.

Wisden, of course, is primarily a book of records, and shows in these obituaries its uncanny sense of them. Achievers may be found here not only of such esoteric sporting accomplishments as the only man to score a hundred and a try at Headingley and the only man in history to be out for a duck in a county match at Stourbridge six weeks after receiving an FA Cup winner's medal, but the setter of a world benchmark for grouse shooting, the rider of 250 winners for the Queen Mother and a hunter involved with 33 packs of hounds. The father of the game in Russian Lapland is honoured; likewise Belgium's favourite cricketing Australian.

Nor are the distinctions merely those of a sporting nature. Here commingled are the founders of *Drum* and of the *Whakatane Beacon*, descendants of Oliver Cromwell and of a man who rescued Charles II; survivors of the force that successfully relieved Cecil Rhodes at Kimberley and the column that arrived too late to save Gordon at Khartoum; commander and casualty at the Battle of Jutland, a survivor and a victim of the *Lusitania*, the inventors of the slips cradle, stump-cam and the 'Aerial' fishing reel; winners of the 1911 Cairo Grand National and of the deck quoits 'Ashes'; the British Army's youngest general and the British Museum's oldest ticket holder, the model for Bobby Southcott in Macdonell's *England, Their England* and the author of a Pindaric ode on the 1981 Headingley Test; holders not just of the Victoria Cross, but of the White Eagle of Serbia and of the Russian Order of St Stanislaus with Swords too. Perhaps the rarest distinction of all is surviving a *Wisden* obituary, like Archibald Fargus, who missed a train and thus his date with death at the Battle of Coronel, and Andrew Newell, whose disappearance turned out to have been deliberate but temporary.

Wisden does not tell us everything. Sometimes it is painfully discreet. 'Of the faults of private character that marred Pooley's career and were the cause of the poverty in which he spent the later years of his life,' it remarks of Ted of that ilk, 'there is no need now to speak.' Five murder victims are included, but the death by hanging of the one murderer, Leslie Hylton, goes unmentioned; nor did *Wisden* try to do justice to the writers P.G. Wodehouse, Rupert Brooke, Samuel Beckett, Terrence Rattigan, R. Warren Chetham-Strode (whose *The Guinea Pig* became the first film to use the word 'arse'), and E.W. Hornung (acknowledged as 'a keen cricketer', but mysteriously not as the creator of Raffles, the Amateur Cracksman). *Wisden*'s detailing of death, however, is sometimes surprisingly unflinching. One can admire the chivalry of Dr C.T. Aveling, who died 'answering the appeal of a nervous lady for help', lament the haplessness of Donald Eligon, who succumbed to blood poisoning from a nail in his cricket boot, or wonder at the waste of Paul Brookes, who bowled Bradman as a 16-year-old and perished of wounds seven years later.

Bradman? Though this is not a selection concerned with the giants of the game, they exert a subtle gravitational pull. W.G. Grace makes his presence felt through the many lives he touched: his devoted batmaker, his last surviving grandchild, a fielder whose hand he shook, an umpire whose decision he ignored, a batsman whose identity he challenged, a famous whip who drove him to a match, a journalist who dismissed him for a duck, another journalist who wrote a book about him saving the world from the Martians, and even one perverse enthusiast who nonetheless 'never took the trouble to see W.G. Grace play'.

It is the fame of great players, moreover, that contributes so much to the cricket fever with whom so many of the subjects in this book were stricken, and which endures even in these less reverent times. Nobody could be more deserving of *Wisden*'s tribute than the individual in this compilation most recently born: 28-year-old fireman Jeffrey Wornham. 'As a boy,' reported the Almanack, 'he spent much of the summer dressed in whites on the off chance that he might find a game he could join.' Wornham's approach to school was linear: 'spring term to prepare for cricket, summer term to play it and autumn term to relive the matches'. Nothing much changed in adulthood: he had spent much of the winter's day that he died knocking in a new bat. Mourners at his funeral in 2005 heard the strains of the BBC's cricket signature tune, 'Soul Limbo'. Above all, this is a book about the enduring appeal of cricket which someone like Jeffrey Wornham personifies. *Vita brevis*, for sure, but *cricket longa*.

Gideon Haigh

Note

The source of the obituaries included in this book is the edition of *Wisden* for the year after the death of the individual concerned (for instance the obituary for Sir George Abell, who died in 1989, appears in *Wisden* 1990). Some mistakes in the original entries have been silently corrected.

ABELL, SIR GEORGE EDMOND BRACKENBURY, KCIE, OBE, who died on January 11, 1989, aged 84, was an all-round sportsman and distinguished member of the Indian Civil Service, serving as private secretary to the last two Viceroys – Lord Wavell and Lord Mountbatten. A right-hand bat and wicket-keeper, he was in the Oxford XI in 1924, 1926 and 1927, as well as captaining the University at rugby and winning a third Blue for hockey. He appeared for Worcestershire 34 times between 1923 and 1938, as his Indian service allowed, his two centuries for them coming in 1925 and 1935.

ABERDARE, THE THIRD BARON (CLARENCE NAPIER BRUCE), who died on October 4, 1957, aged 72, was one of the best all-round sportsmen of his time. His death was caused by drowning after his car fell over a precipice in Yugoslavia into three feet of water in a river bed. As the Hon. C.N. Bruce, he was in the Winchester XI of 1904 and would have gained his Blue at Oxford as a Freshman but for illness. Against Cambridge at Lord's in 1907 he scored only five runs, but the following year his 46 in the Dark Blues' first innings was second top score.

A fine batsman who hit the ball hard with perfect timing, due mainly to splendid wristwork, he first appeared for Middlesex in 1908 and played his last match for them in 1929. In all first-class games he scored 4,316 runs, at an average of 28.96. He won most honours at racquets, for he was the Winchester first string in 1903–4; won the Public Schools championship in 1904; played for Oxford v. Cambridge in 1905–8; won the Oxford University Silver Racquet in 1907; won the Amateur Championship in 1922 and 1931;

was ten times Doubles Champion; was Champion of the U.S.A. in 1928 and 1930.

At tennis, Bruce was U.S.A. Amateur Champion in 1930 and of the British Isles in 1932 and 1938. He played 18 times for Great Britain in the Bathurst Cup and six times won the Coupe de Paris. He carried off the M.C.C. Gold Prize on five occasions and nine times won the Silver Prize. He also excelled at golf, playing for Oxford against Cambridge from 1905 to 1908, was a good footballer and a capital shot.

In 1937 he was appointed chairman of the National Advisory Council in connection with the Government scheme for improving the physical fitness of the nation. For 20 years he was a member of the International Olympic Executive and he played a big part in organising the 1948 Games in London. In his later years he devoted himself closely to work for the Order of St John of Jerusalem and the St John Ambulance Association, and was a member of the executive committee of the National Playing Fields Association. He succeeded to the title in 1929.

ABRAHAM, DR ARTHUR, who died at Whitley Bay, on June 2, 1922, aged 69, was at one time a well-known cricketer in Ireland, playing for Leinster against the South of England, when his resemblance to his twin brother led W.G. Grace to protest against him taking a second innings. He developed into a good wicket-keeper and batsman, and played county cricket for both Durham and Northumberland. In two seasons, also, he took part in the Scarborough Festival.

ABRAHAM, JACOB, believed to have been the first professional cricketer Northampton produced, died in March 1914, at the age of 82. From 1856 until 1868 he was coach at Exeter College, Oxford. He appeared once or twice for XXII of Northamptonshire against the England XI, but without pronounced success. He was married four times, and his widow has lost four husbands.

AINLEY, ANTHONY, who died on May 3, 2004, aged 71, was an actor and a keen club cricketer for The Stage and London Theatres C.C. 'He was an eccentric and very effective opening bat who appeared in full body padding, sunblock, helmet and swimming goggles,' according to his fellow-actor Christopher Douglas, 'and he had a penchant for charging down the track and smashing the ball back over the bowler's head.' Ainley followed his father Henry on to the stage, but found his greatest success on television as The Master, the arch-enemy of Doctor Who, in the 1980s. At one club game at the time, Ainley's fame preceded him, and the *Sutton & Cheam Herald* ran a headline above its match report proclaiming that 'Inter-Galactic Terror' had been visited upon Surrey. A complex character, he usually took his cricket teas alone in his car – possibly because, according to one report, he 'despised cheeses of all kinds'.

AIRD, RONALD, MC, died at his home at Yapton on August 16, 1986, aged 84. Until he was over 80 he had been a very fit man, playing golf regularly and constant in his attendance at race meetings, but in the last two or three years his health had failed, his activities had been sadly restricted, and it was clear to his friends that one who had always been so full of life had now ceased to enjoy it.

Good cricketer though he was, Ronny Aird will always be chiefly remembered for his work at Lord's, which covered first to last 60 years. Appointed Assistant Secretary in 1926 when W. Findlay was promoted to Secretary, he continued to serve under Col. Rait Kerr and himself succeeded as Secretary in 1952. He retired in 1962, but was President in 1968–69 and a Trustee from 1971 to 1983, when he became a Life Vice-President, remaining active on the committee almost to the end. I can remember Lord Cornwallis, who as an ex-President and a Trustee was in a position to know, saying of him as far back as 1950, when he was still only Assistant Secretary: 'No one realises how much that man has done for Lord's.'

It was never Aird's way to seek the limelight. His name seldom appeared in the press. He was not responsible for any startling reforms or innovations. But as one of the papers said after his death, Lord's was never a happier place than during his secretaryship. There was an aura of happiness and it was a joy just to be there, whatever the occasion: all the staff in the pavilion, the tennis-court or elsewhere greeted one as an old friend.

Like many another good strokeplayer, he took some time to acclimatise himself to first-class cricket. Altogether for Hampshire between 1921 and 1938 he scored 3,603 runs with an average of 22.24. Later he was for many years the county's President. A natural games player, he was in two Eton racquets pairs which reached the final at Queen's and in 1922 was second string to R.H. Hill at Cambridge: they won the doubles but Aird lost his single. In 1923 he was first string and won both his matches. Later he concentrated on tennis and became especially formidable at Lord's, where he won the Silver Racquet six times between 1933 and 1949. In the challenge for the Gold Racquet he was defeated twice by Lord Aberdare and four times by W.D. Macpherson, both amateur champions. At Cambridge he was virtually promised a soccer Blue if he would learn to head the ball, but he found that this, especially when the ball was wet, gave him such headaches that he did not think it worth it. In later life he was a National Hunt Steward.

He was a man of wide and varied talents and interests, so varied that few of his friends can have been aware of them all, just as few knew the details of his war record. They knew of course that he had been a major in the Royal Tank Regiment, that he had won the Military Cross in the desert and been wounded. They did not know that he had been in almost a record number of tanks that were totally destroyed or that twice he had been the only survivor; that he had been wounded twice, once severely, and that on both these occasions his one thought had been to get back to active service as soon as possible. Few of his friends can have known the full story, but none will be surprised when he hears it.

ALCOCK, CHARLES WILLIAM, JP, who was born at Sunderland on December 2, 1842, died at Brighton on February 26, 1907. He was educated at Harrow, but, not enjoying very good health, did not obtain a place in the XI. In later years, however, he played occasionally for the Gentlemen of Essex, the Butterflies, Harrow Wanderers and Incogniti, and once had the curious experience of captaining France against Germany in a match at Hamburg. *Scores and Biographies* describes him as a steady bat, a fair change fast bowler, and an excellent long stop or long field. On February 6, 1872, on the strong recommendation of Mr V.E. Walker, he was appointed secretary to the Surrey County C.C., a position he held until the time of his death. Of his work for Surrey cricket it would be difficult to speak too highly, for he was at all times both willing and anxious to do all in his power to further its welfare. He was a most voluminous writer on the game, and in 1882 founded *Cricket*, of which he was editor from the first issue until the day of his death. For 29 years he edited *James Lillywhite's Cricketers' Annual*, and was the chief contributor to *Surrey Cricket: Its History and Associations*, published in 1902. For many years he arranged the fixture-list of teams visiting England, and it was due principally to him that the first meeting between England and Australia in this country – at The Oval in 1880 – took place. Mr Alcock's connection with Association Football was so prominent that it is not too much to say that he more than anyone else made the game. He captained England against Scotland in 1875, and it was under his leadership that the Wanderers won the Football Association Cup in 1872 and in four subsequent years. He was Hon. Secretary of the Football Association from 1867 until 1890, secretary from 1891 until 1896, and a vice-president from the last-mentioned year until his death.

ALEXANDER OF TUNIS, HAROLD RUPERT LEOFRIC GEORGE, Field-Marshal, Earl, who died on June 16, 1969, aged 77, was in the

Harrow XI of 1910, taking part in Fowler's Match, which Eton won at Lord's by nine runs. When Harrow were set 55 to win, R. St L. Fowler bowled his off-breaks with such telling effect that he took eight wickets for 23, the innings being all over for 45. Alexander, then the Hon. H.R.L.G. Alexander, obtained three Eton wickets for seven runs in the first innings and two for 33 in the second. In 1956, he was President of M.C.C. He earned great military distinction in both World Wars, and was later Governor General of Canada and Minister of Defence.

ALLEN, SIR RICHARD WILLIAM, who died at his London home on July 17, 1955, aged 88, was in 1899 one of the founders of Bedfordshire County C.C., of which he was Hon. Secretary until 1919 and President from 1953 till his death. At one time President of the Institution of Mechanical Engineers, he was awarded the CBE in 1918 and knighted in 1942.

ALLWORK, MATTHEW JULIAN, was killed in a helicopter crash in Dubai on March 26, 2003, aged 39, while filming a horse race. Allwork was an innovative cameraman, credited with the invention of the stump-cam.

ALPEN, GEORGE R., one of the best-known cricketers of Belgium, has been killed in the War, but no particulars are obtainable. He was an Australian by birth. (1917)

ALVERSTONE, THE FIRST VISCOUNT, Richard Everard Webster, who was born on December 22, 1842, died at Winterfold, Cranleigh, Surrey, on December 15, 1915. He was educated at King's College, London, and Charterhouse, and was in the latter XI in 1861, when it was said of him: 'Is a good long-field, and with practice will become a fair bat.' He never made a name for himself as a cricketer, but played at least once for the Gentlemen of Devonshire. In 1878 he became a member of the M.C.C., was the Club's President in 1903, served on the Committee 1904–07 and 1909–11, and in July, 1909, succeeded Mr William Nicholson as one of the Trustees. Since May, 1895, he had been President of the Surrey County C.C., and in 1902, in conjunction with Mr C.W. Alcock, edited *Surrey Cricket: Its History and Associations*. At Cambridge, he was a notable athlete, and in 1865 won the mile and two-mile races against Oxford. He was Attorney-General 1885–92 and 1895–1900, and Lord Chief Justice from 1900 to 1913, when he retired through ill-health. With his death the title becomes extinct.

ANDERSON, JOHN CORBET, who was born at Rothesay, Isle of Bute, January 17, 1827, died at Croydon on January 3, 1907, when within a fortnight of completing his 80th year. He will always be remembered on account of the series of fine lithographs of cricketers which he published about 50 or 60 years ago. Mr Anderson was an antiquarian of world-wide fame, and at the time of his death was the oldest ticket holder in the British Museum Reading Room. His best-known work is *Croydon Church, Past and Present*.

APPLEYARD, JACK, one of the best-known faces in Yorkshire cricket circles, died in hospital after a long illness on August 20, 1975, aged 77. Thousands will remember him as the man who brought Sunday cricket to a sports-starved public during the Second World War. It was in 1940 that Appleyard first organised Sunday cricket at Roundhay Park, Leeds, a natural amphitheatre. The games were extremely popular with Test stars attracting as many as 70,000 to one game. Over the year Jack Appleyard's matches raised more than £20,000 for charity and cricketers' benefits. Probably the greatest team of all turned out for the Hedley Verity memorial match in 1944 when 18 Internationals played and Wilfred Rhodes and Emmott Robinson were the umpires.

The Red Cross, Leeds Infirmary, the National Playing Fields

Association, Yorkshire Association of Boys' Clubs and the Cancer Research were among organisations to benefit. Among Yorkshire cricketers whose benefits received handsome donations from match proceeds were W. Barber, W.E. Bowes, T.F. Smailes, Sir Leonard Hutton, J.H. Wardle, Bob Appleyard and F.A. Lowson. Jack Appleyard began in the clothing industry at 13, putting tickets on garments and eventually owned a business that still prospers.

ARROWSMITH, JAMES WILLIAMS, head of the well-known firm of publishers, died at Bristol on January 19, 1914. He was born at Worcester on November 6, 1839, and was always keenly interested in cricket and other sports. For many years he was on the Committee of the County Club, and he was Chairman of the Gloucestershire County Ground Company. Among the many cricket books published by his firm may be mentioned *Cricket* by W.G. Grace; *Kings of Cricket* by Richard Daft; *Gentlemen v. Players* by F.S. Ashley-Cooper; *Cricket Stories* by C.W. Alcock; and *At the Sign of the Wicket* by E.B.V. Christian. Mr Arrowsmith played a great part in the public life of Bristol, and his death caused a gap which will be very difficult to fill.

ASHLEY-COOPER, FREDERICK SAMUEL, unrivalled as an authority on cricket history, died on January 31, 1932, at his home at Milford, Surrey. He was born in London on March 2, 1877, and so had not quite completed his 55th year. From his earliest days he was troubled with poor health and consequently did not follow any profession and yet his unvarying researches and his literary output involved an amount of labour which might well have deterred the most robust of men. His enthusiasm, however, carried him through from these early days when, helped by his friend H.T. Waghorn, an officer of the Reading Room at the British Museum, he spent several years going through, in his search for cricket matter, the newspapers and magazines printed up to the years of 1830.

In this devotion to the history of the game, he was in the succession of the Rev. James Pycroft who, born in 1813, was author of *The Cricket Field*, and of Mr Arthur Haygarth (born in 1825), the compiler of that wonderful work *Scores and Biographies*. Such was Ashley-Cooper's amazing energy that altogether he brought out 103 books and pamphlets on the game dealing with cricket in England, Australia, South Africa, New Zealand, India and other places, besides a very large amount of matter including 40,000 biographical and obituary notices, every production of his pen, moreover, being characterised by phenomenal accuracy to secure which he spared neither time nor trouble.

Among his works were two brought out in conjunction with Lord Harris, *Lord's and the M.C.C.* (dedicated to King George) and *Kent Cricket Matches 1719–1880*, and one with P.F. Warner, *Oxford and Cambridge at the Wicket*. Other products of his pen were *Cricket Highways and Byways, Curiosities of First-Class Cricket, Eton and Harrow at the Wicket, Gentlemen v. Players, E.M. Grace, Cricketer, W.G. Grace, Cricketer, Hambledon Cricket Chronicle*, a new edition of Pycroft's *Cricket Field*, and *Scores and Biographies, XV*, this last being a monumental piece of biography based in the first place upon notes left by Mr Arthur Haygarth and by innumerable additions brought up to date.

Mr Ashley-Cooper edited the newspaper, *Cricket*, for five years and in 1920 he held the Secretaryship of the Nottinghamshire County C.C. He was responsible for more than 30 years for 'Births and Deaths' and 'Cricket Records' in *Wisden*, which latter section of the Almanack had grown from two pages in 1887 to 61 pages in last year's edition. In the course of his career he had gathered a unique collection of cricket books and pictures. For this fortunately he found in Sir Julien Cahn a purchaser a month or two before he died, so the splendid library was not dispersed. Early in 1931, Ashley-Cooper took a trip to the West Indies but derived no benefit from the voyage. Indeed, his health became worse and his sight failed so badly that in the autumn he had to abandon all work. A most modest and kindly man, he was always ready to give from his wonderful store of cricket history to anyone who asked his help and grudged no time spent in satisfying such requests.

To those associated in the production of *Wisden's Almanack*, the passing of Ashley-Cooper is naturally felt as a personal loss. Year by year he had spared no endeavour to make the list of 'Births and Deaths' as complete as possible, conducting an enormous correspondence on the subject and searching the columns of practically every paper he could obtain to bring his information up to date and to eliminate any error. Equally zealous was he in his pursuit of any happening in the game of sufficient importance to be included in 'Cricket Records'. All this labour he performed with a measure of enthusiasm which never flagged even when the shadows were gathering and he knew his days were numbered. Such devotion as his to the game of cricket could not have been surpassed. It should be recognised by the powers that be in the making of arrangements such as will ensure the enlightened continuance of his life's work.

ASHTON, ACTING SQUADRON LEADER CLAUDE THESIGER, the triple Cambridge Blue and England Association football international, was killed on active service on October 31, 1942, in a disaster which also caused the death of Squadron Leader R. de W.K. Winlaw, another Old Wykehamist and double Light Blue.

The youngest of three sons of Mr H.S. Ashton, President of the Essex County Club from 1936, who in turn captained Cambridge cricket XIs and were together in the 1921 team, Claude became the best known. By a strange change of fortune Gilbert and Hubert each led his side to victory over Oxford by an innings, but Claude experienced extreme ill-luck in 1923. Oxford batted all the first day, and during the night a severe thunderstorm with a deluge of rain completely altered the conditions at Lord's, with the result that Cambridge were dismissed twice and beaten on the Tuesday by an innings and 227 runs, the most overwhelming defeat in the whole series of University matches and the three most decisive results to occur consecutively. In this exasperating engagement Claude Ashton, with 15, alone got double figures in the first innings of 59, while in the follow-on his 21 came next best to G.O. Allen's 28. G.T.S. Stevens and R.H.B. Bettington, the Australian Oxford captain, in turn found the drying turf exactly suited to their spin bowling. So, after two great victories under his brothers, Claude Ashton finished his University career in dismal circumstances.

At Winchester, Claude Ashton was captain of cricket, football, racquets and fives. Business prevented him from giving much time to county cricket, but he played some superb innings for Essex, notably in 1934. In an astonishing match at Brentwood with Kent, who scored 803 for four wickets – Ashdown putting together the Kent record of 332 – Claude Ashton, not out 71, showed that he retained his batting form. What a return to the Essex team after five years' absence from county cricket, but two of the wickets fell to him at a cost of 185 runs. Following immediately on this he made 118 against Surrey at Brentwood, helping O'Connor put on 287 for the fifth wicket, an Essex record, in a total of 570, which brought victory by an innings and 192. Altogether in first-class cricket from 1921 to 1938 he was credited with an aggregate of about 5,000 runs at an average of 25, took 139 wickets with his medium-pace bowling, and held 117 catches – he always fielded brilliantly.

Claude Ashton gained perhaps higher fame at Association football than at cricket. He could not lead his side against Oxford when captain at Cambridge in his third year in the XI, but was a grand player, and for Corinthians in Cup ties he occupied every position in the forward and half-back lines. He also appeared at full-back and kept goal for The Casuals. A prominent figure in many matches, he went through some terrific Cup-tie struggles against the best professional teams, and he earned international honours as

centre-forward in October 1925 against Ireland at Belfast, where he
captained England. He played in 13 amateur internationals.

For Cambridge he twice played hockey against Oxford. The three
brothers occupied the inside-forward positions for Old Wykehamists
in Arthur Dunn Cup ties. Born on February 19, 1901, Claude Ashton
died at the age of 41, leaving a widow and three children.

ASHTON, GILBERT, MC, who died at Abberley, Worcestershire, on
February 6, 1981, was the eldest and also the last survivor of three
brothers who played together for Cambridge and captained the
University in three successive years, a record they share with the
Studds. All three were soccer Blues (Gilbert captained Cambridge
and the youngest, Claude, was a full international) and both Hubert
and Claude were hockey Blues as well. A still older brother, Percy,
was good enough to play for Essex after losing an eye in the Great
War. Can any other family equal this record? Gilbert was in the
Winchester XI in 1914 and 1915, when he was captain, and then
went into the Royal Field Artillery, where he won the MC and was
later wounded. No one in after years watching from the boundary
would have realised that he had lost his left thumb: neither in his
batting nor his fielding could one detect any trace of this handicap.
He got his Blue as a freshman in 1919, retained it in 1920 and was
captain in 1921. This 1921 side is often spoken of as the best
University side of this century, though it could be argued that the
1920 side was as strong, but in neither was Gilbert's right to a place
in any doubt. He bent low over his bat in his stance, but was a fine,
aggressive stroke-player and a particularly good cutter and hooker.
He was also a beautiful cover-point.

Almost as soon as he went down he had, in a crisis, to take over
the Headmastership of Abberley Hall, which he retained for 40
years and which was under him one of the most sought-after
preparatory schools in England. For some years he used to play when
possible for Worcestershire in the holidays and did enough to show

what a difference he would have made could he have played regularly: his last appearance was in 1936. In 1922 he made 125 and 84 against Northamptonshire at Worcester. But probably his most notable performance was at Eastbourne in August, 1921, when A.C. MacLaren's XI (of which he was the last survivor) inflicted the first defeat on Armstrong's great Australian side. Dismissed for 43 and going in again 131 down, MacLaren's side at once began to lose wickets and it was Gilbert who, in a brilliant little innings of 36, showed for the first time in the match that the Australian bowlers were not invincible. He paved the way for the splendid partnership of 154 between his brother Hubert and that great South African cricketer, Aubrey Faulkner, which made possible a sensational victory by 28 runs.

In addition to his work as a schoolmaster, he was a magistrate and took a considerable part in public life in Worcestershire, but he never lost his interest in cricket and in particular served for years on the committee of the County C.C., being its President from 1967 to 1969.

ASHTON, SIR HUBERT, MC, who died on June 17, 1979, aged 81, was a batsman who must have taken a high place had he been able to continue in first-class cricket. After two years in the Winchester XI, where he was captain in 1916 and had an outstanding record each year, he served in France from April 1917 and was not demobilised until August 1919. Going up to Cambridge, he made 32 and 62 against Essex next summer in the first match, but such was the competition for places that he was not given another chance until the last home match, when he scored 236 not out against the Free Foresters in four hours; at that time a record both for Cambridge and Fenner's. This made his place secure and he retained it for three seasons, scoring 2,258 runs with an average of 64.51 and each year heading the averages and playing for the Gentlemen at Lord's.

In 1921 he made 118 against Oxford, and in 1922, when he was captain, was 90 not out when he declared the innings closed, thus depriving himself of the chance of scoring a century in successive

Varsity matches. Despite all he did for Cambridge, he is perhaps best remembered for the part he played in the famous victory of MacLaren's XI over the Australians at Eastbourne in 1921. When he and G.A. Faulkner came together in the second innings four wickets were down, and 71 runs were still needed to save an innings defeat; together they added 154, and the Australians were beaten. Coming down from Cambridge in 1922, he joined the Burmah Oil Company. He was not seen again in English cricket until 1927, and rarely thereafter captured his old form. He played soccer for Cambridge for three years and hockey for one. He was one of three brothers who captained Cambridge in consecutive years; a fourth, Percy, was good enough to make runs for Essex despite the loss of an eye in the Great War. Sir Hubert was MP for Chelmsford from 1950 to 1964, president of M.C.C. in 1960, Chairman of Essex from 1941 to 1955, and President from 1955 to 1970. He was knighted in 1959.

ASHTON, HUBERT SHORROCK, father of the three Cambridge captains, Hubert, Gilbert and the late Claude T. Ashton, died on June 10, 1943, in his 82nd year. A strong supporter of cricket, he was president of the Essex County Club from 1936 until his death. Keenly interested in the welfare of the working youth of London, Mr Ashton two years before the war secured the lease of a 50-acre area at Woodford, Essex, and was mainly responsible for having it turned into a modern sports field, with a play-ground for the younger children. The Duke and Duchess of Gloucester formally opened the ground, which is called the Ashton Playing Fields, and planted trees to commemorate the occasion. Mr Winston Churchill and Mr Ramsay MacDonald attended the ceremony.

ASTON, LT-COL. CHARLES, CBE, who died in October 1989, aged 96, was a Manchester-born Arabist of distinction who took part in hazardous desert operations during the Second World War and was a talented all-round games-player. He made no major impact at

Oxford, but became a founder member of the wandering cricket club, the Stragglers of Asia, whose members were required to have served six years in the armed forces east of Suez.

ASTOR OF HEVER, COLONEL LORD (JOHN JACOB ASTOR), First Baron, who died in hospital in Cannes on July 19, 1971, aged 85, was President of M.C.C. in 1937. He was in the Eton XI as an opening batsman in 1904 and 1905 and in the first year, despite an innings of 81 not out, was on the losing side against Winchester. Though he did not get a Blue at Oxford, he later assisted Buckinghamshire. A journalist, he became proprietor of *The Times* and was for years President of the Newspaper Press Fund and of the Press Club.

AUTY, KARL ANDRE, who died in Chicago on November 30, 1959, aged 81, was the owner of an outstanding cricket book collection. Educated at Wheelwright Grammar School, Dewsbury, and on H.M.S. *Conway Training Ship*, he accomplished a Military and General course at the Sorbonne, Paris, and obtained a B.Sc. at Nottingham. He was an active participant in cricket until his late 60s in New England, B.C., and in North America. In the 1930s he published a weekly newspaper, *The British American*, and for some years issued a cricket annual containing full details of Chicago cricket. He was celebrated for his Christmas cards, one of which included the following information: 'It is interesting to note that a Surrey (England) team on its way to play exhibition games in Paris in 1789 was at Dover ready for the crossing, but turned back when met there by their host, the Duke of Dorset, H.B.M. Ambassador, who had fled from Paris before the coming outbreak of the French Revolution. Otherwise this would have been the first team ever to leave Britain's shores to play cricket abroad, thus depriving the 1859 team of that distinction.'

AVELING, DR C.T., whose name will be familiar to a great many Metropolitan cricketers, met with a tragic end on September 5, 1902. Whilst bathing at Helston, Cornwall, he was answering the appeal of a nervous lady for help, when he died of heart disease. He was well-known in connection with the Clapton Club, and had been for some years a member of the Surrey County C.C.

AZIZ, ABDUL, who died, aged 17, during the Final of the Quaid-a-Azam Trophy, played January 16–21, 1959, was a Karachi wicket-keeper. After being struck over the heart by a slow off-break from Dildwar Awan, the Combined Services bowler, he was preparing to receive the next ball when he fell to the ground. He died on the way to hospital without recovering consciousness. This was the first incident of its kind in the Indo-Pakistan sub-continent. Abdul Aziz was a student at S.M. College and an employee of the State Bank.

BADER, GROUP CAPT. SIR DOUGLAS, CBE, DSO, DFC, the famous airman, who died on September 5, 1982, aged 72, was captain of St Edward's School, Oxford, in 1928. A good attacking bat and a useful fast-medium bowler, he later played for the RAF and in 1931 made 65, the top score, for them against the Army, a fixture which in those days had first-class status. He gained greater distinction at rugger, and at the time of the accident the following winter which cost him his legs he was in the running for an England cap.

BAKER, REGINALD LESLIE, who died at Hollywood, California, on December 2, 1953, aged 69, was known as the greatest all-round athlete produced by Australia. He got his Blue at Sydney University for cricket and also for football, athletics and rowing. He took part in 26 different sports, representing Australia at Rugby football and taking part in international polo. Snowy Baker, as he was generally known, fought and lost to the late J.W.H.T. Douglas, who became captain of the England cricket team, for the Olympic middle-weight boxing championship in London in 1908. Though born in Sydney he spent most of his life in America.

BANKS, EDWARD, JP, one of the oldest Kent cricketers, died at Sholden Lodge, near Deal, on January 12, 1910, aged 89. He was born in South Wales on August 12, 1820, but moved into Kent before completing his second year. Ill-health limited his appearances in County Cricket to 10 matches between 1842 and 1846. In the last-mentioned year he appeared for the Gentlemen against the Players at Canterbury, and fielded at Lord's for Alfred Mynn in the first of his single wicket matches with Felix. *Scores and Biographies* (iii-159) says of him, 'Batted in a good free style, and was a most excellent field.' Fuller Pilch recalled that, 'I found him down Sandwich way, where his property lay. He and his youngest brother, Mr William, were the quickest between the wickets I ever did see, and Mr Edward was one of the smartest in the long-field. He was like a thorough-bred horse, for no matter how far the ball was off he would try; and when I sang out, "Go to her, Mr Edward! Go to her!" he would outrun himself almost, and, as sure as ever he got his hands to her, the ball was like a rat in a trap.' His youngest brother, the late Mr W.J. Banks, played occasionally for Kent in 1846 and 1848. The deceased, who was a grandson of Sir Edward Banks, the builder of London Bridge, rode a tricycle as recently as three months before his death.

BARNATO, CAPT. WOOLF, died in a nursing home in London on July 27, 1948, aged 53. Best known for long distance motor-car racing, he occasionally kept wicket for Surrey in the seasons 1928–30. A son of Mr Barney Barnato, the well-known diamond merchant, he was educated at Charterhouse School and Cambridge.

BARRIE, SIR JAMES MATTHEW, BT, OM, who died on June 19, 1937, constantly referred in his writings and speeches to cricket. He was in the XI of the Authors Club who met the Press Club at Lord's in September 1896. In the Press Club XI were H. Vincent Jones, Hubert Preston and S.J. Southerton, all associated for many years with the production of *Wisden*.

BARTLETT, REV. GILBERT HARRISON, who died in a Norwich nursing home on October 10, 1958, aged 76, invented the cradle universally used for fielding practice. When at Cambridge he represented Corpus Christi at rowing and lawn tennis. He was Rector of Fulmodeston, Norfolk, and had been Rector of Cley-next-the-Sea.

BATTCOCK, OLIVER GORDON, who died in Guy's Hospital, London, on September 26, 1970, ten days after his 67th birthday, was reputed to have taken around 6,000 wickets in club and minor county games, with bowling of medium pace, during a cricketing career spanning 50 years. Good length and late out-swing played a big part in his success. He assisted Buckinghamshire from 1923 to 1952, being captain in the last three seasons, and in a Challenge Match of 1938 he dismissed 12 Lancashire batsmen for 65 runs, Buckinghamshire winning in a single innings. He captained Datchet for 25 years, taking over 2,000 wickets for them, and for a number of years led Incogniti on tours abroad. He was also a useful left-handed batsman. As Oliver Gordon, he gained distinction as an actor and producer.

BECKETT, SAMUEL BARCLAY, who died in Paris on December 22, 1989, aged 83, had two first-class games for Dublin University against Northamptonshire in 1925 and 1926, scoring 35 runs in his four innings and conceding 64 runs without taking a wicket. A left-hand opening batsman, possessing what he himself called a gritty defence, and a useful left-arm medium-pace bowler, he had enjoyed a distinguished all-round sporting as well as academic record at Portora Royal School, near Enniskillen, and maintained his interest in games while at Trinity College, Dublin. Indeed, Beckett, whose novels and plays established him as one of the important literary figures of the twentieth century, bringing him the Nobel Prize for literature in 1969, never lost his affection for and interest in cricket.

BEET, GEORGE, achieved his ambition of umpiring in a Test match before he died on December 13, 1946, at his home in Derby. Appointed to the umpires' list in 1929, he stood regularly, and at length was chosen for the England and India Test at Manchester in July, 1946. On the way home by train from that game, Beet was taken seriously ill and rushed to Derby Infirmary for an operation.

From this illness he never recovered. He made his first appearance as wicket-keeper for Derbyshire in 1910, and last played for them in 1922. Very dependable behind the sticks, he also gave useful help with the bat, and in 1919 was second in the Derbyshire averages with 24.80. For several seasons Fred Root was the Derbyshire fast bowler, and the junction of their names in many scores earned the pair the endearing name of 'Beet-root'. During the war George Beet and A. Fowler were the regular umpires in almost every match at Lord's. Beet in several winters went to South Africa as coach. He was 60 years old.

BENTINCK, BERNHARD W., who died on June 27, 1931, aged 53, appeared for Hampshire in 1900 and for some time was President of the Hampshire Hogs C.C. Educated at Winchester, he possessed fine driving powers. Playing for Alton in August 1921, he had the unusual experience of being bowled by a ball (delivered by H. E. Roberts, the Sussex professional) which was deflected on to the wicket through striking and killing a swallow. Mr Bentinck had been a member of M.C.C. for 30 years.

BERESFORD, THE HON. SETON ROBERT DE LA POER HORSLEY, who was born on July 25, 1868, and died at Cap d'Ail on May 28, 1928, aged 59, appeared for Middlesex in two games in 1909. In America he represented New York in Halifax Cup Matches and, playing for Manor Field v. Columbia Oval in 1919, he put up 228 for the first wicket with E.G. Hull. During the South African War, in which he was a special correspondent, he was the first man to enter Kimberley and notify Cecil Rhodes of the approach of the Relief Force.

BILBROUGH, JAMES GORDON PRIESTLEY, who was fatally gassed on November 5, 1944, while engaged on rescue work during a mining accident, was a member of the Eastern Province team in the series of inter-provincial matches played as trials prior to the selection of the 1929 South African team which visited England. He was 34 years of age.

BIRKETT, WILLIAM NORMAN, FIRST BARON, who died on February 10, 1962, aged 78, was a vice-President of Lancashire County C.C. A lover of cricket, he was always in demand at functions connected with the game. He was a regular speaker at the annual dinners of the Cricket Writers' Club, where his turn of phrase, quiet humour and personal charm made him immensely popular. He wrote a little gem of an article, 'The Love of Cricket,' in the 1958 *Wisden*. A very distinguished member of the legal profession, he gained fame in turn as a K.C., Judge of the King's Bench Division and Lord Justice of Appeal.

BISHOP, EDWARD BARRY, died on May 24, 2003, aged 79. Ted Bishop was a journalist and author whose main cricketing achievement was to 'liberate' the Singapore Cricket Club after Britain recaptured the colony in 1945. The club had been used as the HQ of the Japanese secret police and Bishop found a bloodstained cricket bat on the steps. He took six wickets in the club's first post-war match and reportedly used the bat for several years thereafter.

BOWEN, EDWARD ERNEST, senior assistant master at Harrow School, met his death whilst on a cycling tour in France. He fell in attempting to mount his machine, and died almost immediately. He was enthusiastic about cricket, and will long be remembered as the author of several spirited and charming songs on the game. As a player he was a stiff bat, a superb field at long-leg, and a useful wicket-keeper. He was educated at Cambridge, but was not in the XI. Mr Bowen, a younger son of the late Lord Bowen, was born at Wicklow, Ireland, March 30, 1836, and died April 8, 1901, aged 65.

BOWRING, CHARLES WARREN, a native of St John's, Newfoundland, who was educated at Marlborough College, died on November 2, 1940, aged 69. He played for Staten Island club in 1907 and 1908 and was well known in American cricket circles. A prominent shipping agent, he was a member of the American Committee of Lloyd's and a director of the British Empire Chamber of Commerce in the United States. He was one of the survivors when the *Lusitania* was sunk in May, 1915.

BRADFORD, BRIG.-GEN. ROLAND BOYS (DURHAM LIGHT INFANTRY), VC, MC. Twice wounded. Born February, 1892; killed first week of December 1917, aged 25. Played Regimental cricket for Durham Light Infantry. At the outbreak of War he was only a subaltern, and at his death the youngest General in the British Army.

BROCKLEBANK, SIR JOHN MONTAGUE, BT, died at his home in Malta on September 13, 1974, aged 59. Chairman of Cunard from 1959 to 1965, he placed the order for the construction of the QE2. In his younger days at Eton and Cambridge he was a talented bowler of quick leg-breaks and top-spinners. He appeared against Harrow at Lord's in 1933 and took four wickets. In the Arab tour of Jersey in 1935 Hugh Bartlett recognised his possibilities and the following year caused a surprise by inviting him to tour with the Cambridge team three weeks before the University match. In nine innings he took 33 wickets, average 18.48. Bowling from a good height and keeping an accurate length, Brocklebank – a nephew of Sir Stanley Jackson – took ten wickets for 139 in the match against Oxford at Lord's and helped Cambridge to victory by eight wickets.

BROOKE, SUB-LIEUT. RUPERT C. (ROYAL NAVAL DIVISION), born at Rugby on August 3, 1887, died at Lemnos of sunstroke on April 23, 1915. In 1906 he was in the Rugby XI, and although he was unsuccessful in the Marlborough match he headed the school's bowling averages with a record of 19 wickets for 14.05 runs each. He had gained considerable reputation as a poet.

BROOKES, PAUL WILSON, a member of the Lord's ground staff, died in St Mary's Hospital on January 27, 1946, from the effect of wounds received when with the Coldstream Guards in Italy. As a County of London schoolboy he headed the batting averages and played against both Eton and Harrow for selected schoolboy teams. When 16 years of age in 1938 he became famous by bowling Don Bradman in the nets at Lord's during practice before the season began. Hooking at a left-hand delivery, Bradman missed the ball, which took his middle stump.

BROWN, ALBERT, who died on April 27, 1995, aged 83, was a fast-medium bowler who played once for Warwickshire, against the Indians in 1932. He was a leading snooker player and reached the semi-finals of the world championship four times, but retired from the game in 1954 when snooker was so much in the doldrums he could not make a living.

BROWN, HERBERT ARTHUR, secretary of Nottinghamshire from 1920 to 1958, died on July 23, 1974, aged 83. His interest in Nottinghamshire covered 60 years and he was a member of the M.C.C. Advisory committee in the early 1920s. A most popular personality, he was known as Uncle Herbert on local children's broadcast programmes and he was Uncle Herbert to the county cricketers. He bore a heavy burden during the Bodyline dispute in 1932–33.

BRYANT, LEONARD ERIC, died on November 28, 1999, aged 63. Eric Bryant was a slow left-arm bowler who played 22 first-class games for Somerset between 1958 and 1960. He walked out of county cricket shortly after being no-balled five times for throwing against

Gloucestershire at Bath by umpire Hugo Yarnold; in an era where the subject was much-discussed, there had been whispers about Bryant's action, especially for his quicker ball, round the circuit. He went back and became a successful businessman in his home town, Weston-super-Mare, and both captain and groundsman of Weston C.C. Tales of his eccentricity are legendary and largely unprintable, the *Weston Mercury* reported fondly after his death, but he is the only Weston player to have taken his cricket gear off, had a shower and then dressed in his ordinary clothes while smoking a lighted cigarette, which at no time left his lips during the whole procedure.

BULLOCK, BURN W., who died suddenly on December 23, 1954, aged 58, scored many runs as a professional for Surrey Second XI between 1921 and 1925, his highest innings being 153 in 1923. As Surrey were specially strong in batting at that time, he could rarely find a place in the first team and in 1926 he became coach and cricket organiser to the late Mr Jimmy White, the millionaire financier. He later returned to the Mitcham Club, for whom he made his first appearance at the age of 15.

BULPETT, CHARLES WILLIAM LLOYD, who died at Nairobi, Kenya, on July 11, 1939, aged 87, played for Rugby against Marlborough at Lord's in 1891, and appeared for Middlesex against Yorkshire there in 1880. He did not gain his cricket Blue at Oxford, but enjoyed a reputation for other sporting activities. Over a level measured mile at Newmarket in 1887 he won a wager of £200 and £400 in bets by walking a mile, running a mile and riding a mile in less than 18 minutes. A year later, at the age of 35, he accomplished the feat again in better time and won a bet of £1,000 to £400. A sound bat and useful fast bowler, he succeeded A.G. Guillemard as Hon. Secretary of the Butterflies C.C. and was, in his turn, followed by C.F.H. Leslie.

BURROWS, ARTHUR, the oldest cricketer who had played in a match of note at Lord's, died at The Larches, Beckenham, on September 13, 1908, in his 97th year. He was born on August 26, 1812, and played for Winchester against Eton at Lord's in 1829, when he scored 0 not out and 17. He was known as The Father of the English Bar, being the oldest practising barrister in England, and until a short time before his death went to his chambers in Lincoln's Inn regularly two or three times a week.

BUSH, RONALD GEORGE, who died on May 10, 1996, aged 87, was one of two men (along with Alan Clark of Wellington) to have played in winning teams in both New Zealand's traditional inter-provincial cricket and rugby competitions: the Plunket Shield and the Ranfurly Shield. He was a seam bowler who played ten first-class matches for Auckland in the 1930s. During a rugby tour of Japan, he is said to have given his boots to the son of the Tokyo University captain, who later became commandant of a PoW camp in Malaya. When an officer answered 'Yes' to the question 'You know Ron Bush?', conditions in the camp improved immediately.

BUTLER, THE REV. ARTHUR GRAY, died at Glenfinnan, Torquay, on January 16, 1909, in his 80th year. He was in the Rugby XI in 1847 and 1848, being captain in the latter year, and was above the average as a batsman. For some years he was an assistant master at Rugby under Dr Temple, and was afterwards appointed first headmaster of Haileybury. He was Butler of 'Butler's Leap' at Rugby and winner of the racquet pairs at Oxford in 1855. He is said to have been the only man who ever jumped the river Cherwell, a tributary of the Thames at Oxford.

BYASS, ROBERT WILLIAM, who died at his home in London on August 22, 1958, aged 97, had been a member of M.C.C. since 1881. An enterprising batsman and useful medium-pace bowler, he was in the

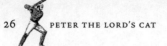

Eton XI in 1878 and 1879, but failed to gain a Blue at Oxford. He played in some matches for Free Foresters. He became head of the wine-shipping firm of Gonzalez, Byass and Co., who in 1954 dedicated a cask of sherry, believed to be the oldest in the world, to Sir Winston Churchill to mark his 80th birthday.

C

CAKOBAU, RATU SIR EDWARD, who died in Suva, Fiji, on June 25, 1973, aged 64, played for Auckland and when captain of Fiji against a New Zealand touring team in 1937 he hit a century. He played for various teams when in England in 1946, turning out bare-footed in the native Fiji attire. He was President of the Fiji Cricket Association and was manager of the Fiji Rugby football touring team of 1964. Son of King George of Tonga, he became Deputy Prime Minister of Fiji when the colony was granted independence in 1970.

CAKOBAU, RATU SIR GEORGE KADAVULEVU, GCMG, GCVO, who died in Suva on November 23, 1989, aged 77, was the first Fijian to be Governor-General of the then Commonwealth state, and a keen games-player vice-captain of P. A. Snow's 1947–48 Fiji side in New Zealand. An attacking bat with a wide range of strokes, a steady medium-pace bowler who moved the ball and gained bounce on responsive pitches, and able to keep wicket, the most successful all-rounder of the side, averaging 21 with the bat and 24 wickets at 24 runs apiece on tour (which included two matches in Fiji). His 65 not out against Wellington was largely responsible for Fiji's first win over a major province. In 1987, ICC approved first-class status for the five major provincial matches, giving 75-year-old Sir George great satisfaction at gaining such confirmation of his cricket quality and making him the oldest cricketer to be graded so. His first-class career record, from four matches, thus became 176 runs at an average of 25.14 and five wickets at 52.00 from 85 overs. He had missed the last four matches of the tour after having a toe broken while batting at Napier against Hawke's Bay – the only such injury sustained by the several members of the team who played barefoot. Ratu

(High Chief) Sir George was a major figure in Fiji who made a considerable impact on his travels, with a native personality sharpened by Antipodean irreverence stemming from his time at Sydney's Newington College, and Wanganui Technical College in New Zealand.

He captained the Fijian rugby team to New Zealand in 1939, and in 1952 and 1954 he managed similar tours to Australia. He served gallantly during the Second World War with the Fiji Infantry Regiment fighting the Japanese in the Solomon Islands, and his status as great-grandson of Ratu Ebenezer Seru Cakobau, the only King of Fiji, made him a natural choice as Governor-General in 1973 when the independent state looked for a royal representative from its own people. He is widely credited with helping to retrain the Fijian community during the coup against the elected government in 1987, but was then physically no longer strong enough to play a leading role in uneasy times. He was appointed GCMG in 1973, GCVO in 1977, and in 1982 was given the rare honour of the Royal Victorian Chain, conferred on him by The Queen on her visit to his island of Bau.

CALDER, HARRY LAWTON, who died in Cape Town on September 15, 1995, aged 94, was both the youngest ever and the oldest surviving *Wisden* Cricketer of the Year. Calder was chosen as one of the School Bowlers of the Year in 1918 when there was no regular selection because of the war. He was in the Cranleigh XI for five years as a bowler of varied medium-paced spinners. But he played little cricket after leaving school, when he went to South Africa, and did not know he had ever been a Cricketer of the Year until he was tracked down in 1994. The Calder story appeared in the 1995 *Wisden*, page 275.

CAMPBELL, THOMAS, the well-known South African cricketer, was killed in the Natal railway accident which occurred to the up-mail train from Durban at Milndale early on the morning of October 5, 1924. He was born in Natal on February 9, 1882, and was thus over 42 years at the time of his death. As a batsman he was of small account, although in a Test match against England at Durban in 1909–10 he played an innings of 48, but as a wicket-keeper he gained much note. He made his first appearance for the Transvaal in Currie Cup matches in 1906–7, and four seasons later toured Australia as a member of the South African Team. With Percy Sherwell's services at command, however, he took part in none of the Test matches. In 1909–10, when South Africa won the rubber at England's expense, he took part in four games, and in 1912 he visited England. Whilst in this country rheumatism in the hands prevented him from showing his best form, and the only time he took part in one of the Triangular Tournament matches was when he played against England at Lord's.

Remembering the circumstances of his death, it is interesting to recall that on December 16, 1916, he fell out of the Cape mail train from Johannesburg. He was picked up in an unconscious condition by the driver of a goods train and was found to be suffering from concussion of the brain and other head injuries. He was removed to Krugersdorp Hospital, and for some time it was doubtful if he would recover.

CANNON, JAMES, for 65 years with M.C.C. at Lord's, died on April 20, 1949, aged 82. He started as a ball-boy for the tennis courts when 12 and held the horses for members when they visited the ground. Gradually he climbed the ladder, becoming boot-boy in the cricket dressing-rooms, and then went into the office where for many years he was chief clerk. A small, popular figure, Jimmy Cannon was given the title King of Lord's, by Sir Pelham Warner. A keen gardener, he was recognised by hundreds of people by his straw-hat and button-hole of sweet-peas, rose or carnation. On his retirement in 1944, he was elected an honorary member of M.C.C.

CARR, JAMES LLOYD, who died on February 26, 1994, aged 81, was an author and publisher who ran a one-man business from his home in Kettering. Two of J.L. Carr's eight novels were short-listed for the Booker Prize; another, *A Season in Sinji*, is arguably the best of all novels with a cricketing backdrop. He also published, in 1977, *Carr's Dictionary of Extraordinary English Cricketers*, with an enlarged edition in 1983. Factually not for the purist, the book remains a humorous gem. Carr was originally a schoolmaster and enthusiastic club cricketer, whose literary ability surfaced when he was editing the Northamptonshire County League handbook in the 1950s and contributing his own idiosyncratic notes. He was the *Wisden* book reviewer in 1993.

CARR, FLIGHT LIEUT. HARRY LASCELLES, died in a London nursing home after an operation on August 12, 1943. He and his twin brother, sons of Sir Emsley, played in the Clifton XI from 1924 to 1926. They were also in the Rugby football XV. In his third match against Tonbridge at Lord's, Harry Carr played a good forcing innings of 56 on a pitch recovering from rain. A useful wicket-keeper, he appeared occasionally for Glamorgan from 1931 to 1934. He excelled at golf and billiards, representing Cambridge at both these games. A member of the *News of the World* staff with his father, he joined the R.A.F. and served in the intelligence branch for two and a half years until incapacitated by ill-health.

CARTER, THE REV. EDMUND SARDINSON, died at Scarborough on May 23, 1923. Mr Carter will be remembered not so much for what he did in the cricket field as for his personality. In whatever company he found himself he could not help being a prominent figure. Retaining as long as his health lasted the keenest interest in the game, he had a better collection of cricket stories than any of his contemporaries except, possibly, E.M. Grace, who could never be persuaded to let his be printed. No doubt the best of Mr Carter's tales are those published in his interview in *Old English Cricketers*, but he had an inexhaustible store. Going up from Durham Grammar School Mr Carter was a double blue at Oxford, playing in the XI in 1866 and 1867 and rowing in the boat in 1867 and 1868. He had no chance of being in the XI in 1868, as a severe attack of pleurisy compelled him to take a sea voyage to Australia. While in Sydney he played for Victoria against New South Wales, and with scores of 16 and 63 (the highest innings on either side) helped to win the game by 78 runs. The match has, in the historic sense, a special interest. In Frank Allan, who took eight wickets for 20 runs and got New South Wales out for 37, Mr Carter saw the first of the long line of great Australian bowlers. I have often wondered whether at the time he had any idea of what Allan's success portended.

CARTER, HORATIO STRATTON, died on October 9, 1994, aged 80. Raich Carter was a lower-order batsman and medium-pace bowler who played three away matches for Derbyshire in June 1946. He had appeared for Durham in 1933 and 1934. He managed only eight runs and two wickets in first-class cricket, but achieved considerably more fame as a footballer. He scored 216 goals in 451 league games with Sunderland, Derby County and Hull City, won one League Championship, two F.A. Cups and 13 England caps (in a career interrupted by the war) and was described by *The Times* on his death as one of the half-dozen geniuses of the game in England. He was one of five England footballers to play first-class cricket for Derbyshire – the others being Billy Foulke, the 21-stone goalkeeper, John Goodall, Ernest Needham and Harry Storer (jnr). He was, though, almost certainly the only man in history to be out for a duck in a county match at Stourbridge six weeks after receiving an F.A. Cup winner's medal.

CASTLE, DENNIS, who died in February 1993, aged 78, counted cricket high among a variety of interests. He was member No. 111 of the

Lord's Taverners and captained the charity's team. Of his two novels, one, *Run Out the Raj*, featured a fictional cricket team in India. He was the first editor of the comic *Radio Fun*.

CAT, PETER (THE), whose ninth life ended on November 5, 1964, was a well-known cricket-watcher at Lord's, where he spent 12 of his 14 years. He preferred a close-up view of the proceedings and his sleek, black form could often be seen prowling on the field of play when the crowds were biggest. He frequently appeared on the television screen. Mr S.C. Griffith, Secretary of the M.C.C., said of him: 'He was a cat of great character and loved publicity.'

CAZALET, MAJOR PETER VICTOR FERDINAND, who died on May 29, 1973, aged 66, was a fine all-round sportsman. In the XI at Eton as opening batsman in 1925 and 1926, he scored 100 not out against Harrow at Lord's in the second year, when he headed the averages with 53.66. Quick on his feet, he timed the ball splendidly, especially his on-side strokes, and possessed a sound defence. Though he gained a Blue at Oxford in 1927, he did not reproduce his earlier form. He also represented the University at racquets, lawn tennis and squash. Between 1927 and 1932 he turned out on occasion for Kent. He showed much promise as a steeplechase jockey till a bad fall ended his career in 1938. He then took to National Hunt training and was in charge of the horses of Queen Elizabeth the Queen Mother for 25 years. Of his 1,100 winners, more than 250 wore the Queen Mother's colours.

CHALK, FLIGHT LIEUT. FREDERICK GERALD HUDSON, DFC, missing from February 1943, was in January officially presumed killed. His tragic and uncertain death at the age of 32 was deplored by all who knew him, and everyone interested in cricket. For Uppingham, Oxford and Kent he batted and fielded so brilliantly that he became an attractive figure whenever he played.

CHETHAM-STRODE, R. WARREN, who died on April 26, 1974, aged 78, was in the Sherborne XI in 1913. He became a playwright, whose most successful work was *The Guinea Pig* in 1946. When serving in the Army in the First World War, he won the MC. His father played for New Zealand in the first team from that country to oppose an England XI, in 1879.

CLARK, ARTHUR HENRY SEYMOUR, who died on March 17, 1995, aged 92, was an engine driver from Weston-super-Mare and one of the most improbable of all county cricketers. Seymour Clark never played the game at all before he was 25, when he was drafted in to keep wicket for a makeshift railwaymen's side. He turned out to be a brilliant natural wicket-keeper, with fantastic reflexes, and quickly became first choice for the Weston town club. Three years later, when the regular Somerset keeper Wally Luckes was ill, Clark was brought in and, though he had trouble getting time off from the railway, played five matches in 1930. He kept magnificently; however, he is mainly remembered for his batting, which was hopeless. Clark thought his highest score in club cricket was three, and two of them came from overthrows. He bought a new bat when he was picked for the county, but hardly ever made contact, failing to score a run in nine innings (though twice at Kettering his partner got out before he could). Peter Smith of Essex tried to give him one off the mark, and produced a ball that bounced twice before it reached him; Clark still got bowled. He was offered a contract for 1931 but thought the Great Western Railway offered more secure employment. 'I got a tremendous kick out of playing for Somerset,' he said later, 'but it seemed sensible to go back to the locos.'

CLARKE, CHARLES FREDERICK CARLOS, born at Welton, Northamptonshire, on April 26, 1853, died at Sunninghill on January 20, 1931. He started the Silwood Cricket Club, which was one of the very few cricket clubs to use white stumps. Closely associated with

Canterbury Week and the famous band of amateur actors the Old Stagers, he was an accomplished actor and musician. A keen all-round sportsman, he had hunted with 33 different packs of hounds.

CLOETE, WILLIAM BRODRICK, was born in 1851 and was drowned in the torpedoing of the *Lusitania* on May 7, 1915. Since 1877 he had been a member of M.C.C., for which he had played in many matches. He was a well-known owner and breeder of racehorses. The best horse he ever owned was Paradox – second to Melton in the Derby in 1885.

CLUES, ARTHUR, who died on October 3, 1998, aged 74, played rugby league for both Leeds and Australia, and club cricket for Leeds C.C. He is believed to be the only man to score both a century and a try at Headlingley.

CLUGSTON, DAVID LINDSAY, died on September 27, 1993, aged 85. Lin Clugston was a left-handed batsman who played six games for Warwickshire between 1928 and 1946. He later became more familiar, until 1988, as the stentorian-voiced ground announcer at Edgbaston who would upbraid small boys for the slightest mischief in an echoing basso profundo. His successor is still sometimes called 'the Cluggie'.

COBB, HUMPHRY HENRY, who died after a long illness on December 13, 1949, played 14 innings for Middlesex in the latter part of the last century, scoring 157 runs. He captained Rosslyn Park F. C. for three seasons from 1896–97 to 1898–99. Born on July 12, 1876, he was at one time President of the Bear Skating Club.

COLE, FREDERICK LIVESAY, an occasional wicket-keeper for Gloucestershire from 1879, when he first appeared at Lord's, died at

Sheffield on July 1, 1941. While he would be a useful cricketer to pass muster with W.G. Grace as captain, a more interesting point than his prowess behind the stumps concerns his age. In *Scores and Biographies* the date of his birth is given as October 4, 1856. This tallied with *Wisden* until 1934, when the year was altered to 1842 – a possible misprint due to re-setting 'Births and Deaths'. Yorkshire papers described how 'he joined the Federal Army when 19 and served for four years under Generals McClellan and Phil Sheridan'; also that during the Franco-Prussian war he was in the siege of Paris and that he was with Sir Archibald Forbes, the war correspondent, in the Russo-Turkish war before being invalided home in 1876. Inquiries at the Bristol Grammar School, where he was said to have been educated, failed to trace him, neither can any mention of his name between 1837 and 1887 be found in the Registers of the Yeovil district, though his birthplace was recorded as Ilminster, together with the date, at the time of his first match at Lord's.

In response to a question in the *Bristol Evening Post*, Mr Harry Wookey wrote that he played 'with Fred Cole for Schoolmasters against Bath Association in 1880, when I was only 17 years of age. Fred Cole was born on October 4, 1856.' Another Bristol cricketer confirmed that opinion. Yet it was asserted in the Yorkshire papers that 'he had three centenarian brothers all living' and that he was 90 when he retired from the Sheffield Gas Company, though no one knew his exact age and thought he was 60: 'George,' one of the 'centenarian' brothers, could not be traced in Bristol.

Fred Cole made plenty of runs in club cricket, and H.E. Roslyn, of the Gloucestershire County Committee, recalls that 'Fred Cole scored the first hundred ever made on our county ground and I kept wicket while he did so' – that was the year before the formal opening in 1889.

COMFORT, PROFESSOR HOWARD, who died in Philadelphia on September 20, 1993, aged 89, spent almost the whole of his life at

Haverford College, Pennsylvania, the last cricket-playing college in the U.S. As a student he made 124 against Merion and in 1925 captained Haverford on a tour of England. He stayed on to become Professor of Classics and founded the C. C. Morris Cricket Library at the college. He was a world authority on Roman pottery and, in the 1960s, was briefly U.S. cultural attaché in Italy.

COWAN, SAMUEL, who collapsed while refereeing a football match at Haywards Heath for the benefit of J.H. Parks on October 6, 1964, and died shortly afterwards, aged 65, had been masseur to Sussex C.C.C. since soon after the Second World War and acted in that capacity with the M.C.C. Team in Australia in 1962–63. Better known as an Association footballer with Denaby United, Doncaster Rovers, Manchester City and Bradford City, he played at centre-half in three matches for England between 1926 and 1931. He captained Manchester City when they won the F.A. Cup in 1933–34 and in two other Cup Finals, afterwards became manager of the club and served as trainer to Brighton and Hove Albion.

COXON, HENRY ('HARRY'), born at New Lenton on August 12, 1847, died at West Bridgford on November 5, 1929, aged 82. For very many years he was the Nottinghamshire scorer, undertaking the duties for the first time in 1867 and, except during the 'Cricket Schism' of 1881, carrying them out regularly from 1870 until the end of 1923. His activities thus extended from the time of George Parr to that of A.W. Carr, and he claimed to have noted every run made for the county by Arthur Shrewsbury – to whom he was distantly related – during that batsman's long and successful career. He was a great authority on angling, on which subject he wrote a treatise, and he invented the 'Aerial' fishing-reel. In 1898 the Notts team gave him a gold pin surmounted with a jewelled fly. He wrote much on sporting subjects, especially cricket and fishing, beginning his journalistic work with the old *Nottingham Review*. In 1924 the match at Trent Bridge between the Second XIs of Nottinghamshire and Lancashire was given to him as a benefit.

CRAIG, ALBERT, 'The Surrey Poet', died after a long illness at 8, Mayflower Road, Clapham, on July 8, 1909, in his 60th year. A Yorkshireman by birth and upbringing, he started life as a Post Office clerk in Huddersfield, but was still a young man when, discovering that verse-making was his forte, he decided to devote his time and energies to celebrating the doings of cricketers and footballers. He was a familiar and welcome figure on the chief grounds in all parts of the country, but especially those of Surrey and Kent. He was possessed of much humour and it was seldom indeed that anyone had the best of him in a battle of wits. His pleasantries, which were never ill-natured, served to beguile many a long wait occasioned by the weather.

CRAWLEY, AIDAN MERIVALE, MBE, who died on November 3, 1993, aged 85, was one of seven members of his family, Harrovians all, to play first-class cricket, and perhaps the most brilliant. His 87 against Eton at Lord's in 1926 was widely regarded as the best innings in the match for many years. In *Wisden*, H.S. Altham called him a beautiful player. In 1928 he broke the Oxford scoring record, with 1,137 runs (average 54.14) and five hundreds, including 167 against Essex and 162 against Surrey. In 1929, he made 204 against Northamptonshire at Wellingborough with ten sixes and 22 fours, apparently having driven to the ground straight from an Oxford ball. For the Gentlemen at Lord's he hit A.P. Freeman over the old free seats on to the Nursery End.

He played 33 matches for Kent, mostly in 1931 and 1932, but his subsequent career took him off in many different directions, most of them distinguished, some contradictory: he was Labour MP for Buckingham (rising to be Under-Secretary of State for Air in 1951) and, having grown disillusioned with nationalisation,

Conservative MP for West Derbyshire. He was also a pioneering documentary film-maker, a fighter pilot, a PoW who staged a spectacular if brief escape, the biographer of de Gaulle and an early TV personality, as presenter of the 1950s series *Viewfinder*. In 1955 he became the first head of Independent Television News, where he encouraged the then novel idea of probing questions, and he was later the first chairman of London Weekend Television. He retained his cricketing connections, was president of M.C.C. in 1972–73, chairman of the National Cricket Association for its first seven years and one of the begetters of the National Village Championship. His perseverance did not always match his versatility and panache. The last years of this handsome, gilded figure were clouded with tragedy: his wife was killed in a car crash and his two sons in a plane crash.

CRAWLEY, LEONARD GEORGE, a member of a notable games-playing family and himself one of the most versatile games-players of his day, died on July 9, 1981, aged 77. Though he was perhaps best known to the general public as for years golfing correspondent of the *Daily Telegraph* and one of the select body of Englishmen who have won a single in the Walker Cup, in which he appeared four times, he might well have been no less distinguished in the cricket world if he had been able to give the time to the game: in addition he had been first string for Cambridge at racquets and he was a fine shot.

Three years in the Harrow XI, he played a memorable innings of 103 at Lord's in 1921, and, getting his Blue at Cambridge as a freshman in 1923, played three years also for them. In 1925 he was 98 not out at lunch against Oxford, needing only two runs to equal the record of his uncle, Eustace Crawley, the only man who had made a century in both the Eton and Harrow and the Varsity match: unfortunately he was out to the first ball after lunch. In 1922, his last year at school, and again in 1923, he had headed the Worcestershire batting averages, in 1923 actually averaging 86, but Lord Harris discovered that neither he nor the leading Worcestershire professional batsman, Fox, was properly qualified and M.C.C. declared both ineligible for the county. This led to a famous scene in the Long Room at Lord's between Lord Deerhurst, the Worcestershire President, and Lord Harris, with J.W.H.T. Douglas, unseen it is thought by the protagonists, mimicking the actions of a boxing referee in the background.

In 1925–26 Crawley went on an M.C.C. tour of the West Indies, then quite a minor affair, and from 1926 to 1937 played for Essex, though never for more than a few matches a season and sometimes not for that. However, in 1932 he averaged 51.87 for them and was asked whether he would be available to go to Australia that winter if wanted. Again in 1937 against Glamorgan at Pontypridd, on his first appearance of the season, he made 118, including five sixes, two of them out of the ground: no one else made 20. But the effort left him so stiff that he was unable to take any further part in the match.

A few weeks later he featured in a bizarre incident against Worcestershire at Chelmsford. Crawley was one of the greatest drivers, straight and to the off, of his day, good enough to force Maurice Tate in his prime to station a man by the screen. On this occasion the visiting captain, the Hon. C.J. Lyttelton, seeing him coming out to open and knowing that, given a chance, he would try to drive the first ball over the screen, instructed the bowler, Perks, to give him one slightly short of a length on the middle stump. Perks produced just the right ball and Crawley's bat struck it when its face was pointing straight upwards to the sky. The ball rose vertically to an astronomical height. A.P. Singleton in the gully put his hands in his pockets and said: 'I'm not taking that.' Lyttelton looked round in desperation and finally said to Singleton, 'Sandy, you've got to take it', whereupon Singleton took his hands out of his pockets and held what in the circumstances was a fine catch.

CRISP, ROBERT JAMES, DSO, MC, who died in Essex on March 3, 1994, aged 82, was one of the most extraordinary men ever to play Test cricket. His cricket, which is only a fraction of the story, was explosive enough: he is the only bowler to have taken four wickets in four balls twice. Born in Calcutta, he was educated in Rhodesia and, after taking nine for 64 for Western Province against Natal in 1933–34, which included his second set of four in four, was chosen for the South Africans' 1935 tour of England. He took 107 wickets on the tour at a brisk fast-medium, including five for 99 in the Old Trafford Test. Crisp played four further Tests against Australia in 1935–36 and appeared eight times for Worcestershire in 1938 without ever achieving a huge amount.

But it is astonishing that he ever found a moment for such a time-consuming game as cricket. He was essentially an adventurer – he had just climbed Kilimanjaro when he got news that he was wanted for the 1935 tour – with something of an attention span problem. Like other such characters, his defining moment came in the Second World War when he was an outstanding but turbulent tank commander, fighting his own personal war against better-armoured Germans in Greece and North Africa. He had six tanks blasted from under him in a month but carried on fighting and was awarded the DSO for outstanding ability and great gallantry. However, he annoyed authority so much that General Montgomery intervened personally and prevented him being given a Bar a year later; his second honour was downgraded to an MC. Crisp was Mentioned in Dispatches four times before being invalided out in Normandy. The King asked if his bowling would be affected. 'No, sire,' he is alleged to have replied. 'I was hit in the head.'

Crisp never did play again and found that the tedium of peacetime presented him with a problem far harder than anything offered by the Germans. He was briefly a journalist for a succession of newspapers, and went back to South Africa where he founded the now firmly-established paper for blacks, *Drum*. But he wanted a magazine about tribal matters rather than something appealing to urban blacks and rapidly fell out with his proprietor. He returned to England, tried mink farming and, for an unusually long time by Crisp standards, worked as a leader-writer on the *East Anglian Daily Times*. While there he wrote two accounts of his war exploits, *Brazen Chariots* (1957) and *The Gods Were Neutral* (1960).

Then he suddenly left and lived in a Greek hut for a year. Told he had incurable cancer, he spent a year walking round Crete, selling accounts to the *Sunday Express*. He died with a copy of the *Sporting Life* on his lap, reportedly having just lost a £20 bet, a risk-taker to the last. Crisp's 276 career wickets came at an average of only 19.88, but statistics are absurd for such a man.

CROCKETT, ROBERT W., the Australian umpire, died on December 12, 1935, aged 72. Born in Melbourne, he was closely connected with Melbourne cricket for many years, and was at work on the club's famous ground when he contracted a chill, as the result of which he passed away. Bob Crockett stood in most of the Test matches during a long period when England teams visited Australia, and was held in high regard by everyone for his accurate decisions. Recognised by cricketers the world over as one of the finest umpires of his time, his quiet demeanour, unfailing good humour and strict impartiality endeared him to all players with whom he came in contact. When failing sight compelled him to give up umpiring, he became a director in a company to make cricket bats at Melbourne out of Tasmanian willow. This experiment proved fairly satisfactory, and provided Crockett with a livelihood for many years. The bats are still being made. So many times did Crockett umpire at the end from which Blackie, the Victorian, bowled, and so many decisions did he give in favour of Blackie, that their combination gave rise to many jests. When the two met in the street, 'Rocketty' would welcome Crockett with 'How's that, Bob?' and the umpire answered with the out signal, raising his hand high in the air. J.B. Hobbs coupled him with Frank Chester as the best umpires he knew, and the Surrey batsman had good opportunities of forming an opinion, because when he was in the M.C.C. team captained by A.O. Jones in 1907, Crockett already held an honoured name for his unfailing care and accuracy. Crockett came to England with the Australian team in 1926 and umpired in one match – Public Schools XV v. The Australians, at Lord's.

Mr P.F. Warner, when asked about Bob Crockett, said: 'A very fine umpire: one of the best I have ever seen. He commanded the respect of everyone, and gained a reputation with English cricketers who, even if they doubted whether they were out, were quite satisfied when they realised that Crockett had made the decision.'

CUMMINGS, JOSEPH, who died from the heat at Pullman, Ill., on June 15, 1913, was born at Durham on July 10, 1861. He went to Chicago in 1886, and, after playing for the Wanderers, identified himself with the Pullman C.C. He was a punishing bat and a good fast bowler. His highest score was 162 for Milwaukee v. Racine College.

CURRIE, SIR DONALD, KCMG, the famous shipowner and philanthropist, who was born at Greenock on September 17, 1825, died at the Manor House, Sidmouth, on April 13, 1909. He was the donor of the Currie Cup, which has been the means of greatly increasing the popularity of the game in South Africa.

CURTIN, JOHN, PRIME MINISTER OF AUSTRALIA, a cricket enthusiast, died on July 4, 1945, aged 60. Notwithstanding his many national activities he maintained a close interest in cricket and often mentioned the game in his speeches. Last year's *Wisden* quoted his memorable remarks regarding Lord's when he became a Freeman of London.

Early in the War he declared that games were not detrimental to the War effort, but a refresher, and he recommended that a series of

Test matches between Australia and England should be played immediately after the War as an effective way of demonstrating to the world the characteristics of the British race. Mr Curtin visited Lord's in 1944, and just before the first 'Victory Test' in May he sent a message to M.C.C. conveying his best wishes for the reopening of a series which he hoped would never again be interrupted.

Flight-Lieut. K. Johnson, a member of the Australian Board of Control, who was in England when the news came that Mr Curtin was dead, said that although a very busy man at Canberra, the headquarters of Australian politics, a long way from cricket centres, Mr Curtin seldom missed an opportunity of watching the game. He was often a spectator at West Australia matches. By his death, cricket in England and Australia lost a very valuable friend and supporter.

D

DALLAS BROOKS, GEN. SIR REGINALD ALEXANDER, who died on March 22, 1966, aged 69, was in the Dover XI from 1912 to 1914 as a batsman and medium-paced bowler. In his last season he headed the School batting figures with 939 runs, of which he scored 187 in an innings against King's School, Canterbury, at an average of 62.62, and was also leading bowler with 36 wickets at 12.94 runs each. In 1919 and 1921 he appeared in a few matches for Hampshire, hitting 107 from the Gloucestershire bowling at Southampton in the first year. A fine all-round sportsman, he captained the Combined Services against touring teams from Australia, South Africa and New Zealand, led them at hockey, at which he played for England against Ireland and France, and captained the Royal Navy at golf. Joining the Royal Marines on his 18th birthday, he earned the DSO in the First World War for his part in the St George's Day raid on Zeebrugge in 1918. He was Governor of Victoria from 1949 to 1963.

DAVIDSON, KENNETH R., who was killed in an airplane crash at Prestwick Aerodrome on December 25, 1954, the day after his 49th birthday, played as a batsman for Yorkshire on a number of occasions from 1933 as amateur and professional. In 1934 he scored 1,053 runs, including an innings of 128 against Kent at Maidstone. Previously he appeared for the Second XI, for Bingley in the Bradford League and for Scotland. Better known as a badminton player, at which he displayed remarkable ability, he went to America in 1935 and was returning to his New York home after a world tour with a U.S.A. team when he met his death.

DAVIES, HARRY DONALD, who was killed in the Munich air crash on February 6, 1958, aged 65, when returning from a football match in Belgrade with the Manchester United team, played in 11 games for Lancashire in 1924 and 1925. His best score was 46 against Kent in the first match. After the War he became a member of the Lancashire County Committee and also a vice-president. He played football for Bolton Wanderers and gained an Amateur International cap for England. For nearly 30 years he wrote for the *Manchester Guardian* under the nom de plume of 'Old International'.

DAVIES, JACK GALE WILMOT, OBE, who died at Cambridge on November 5, 1992, aged 81, was a remarkable man who achieved many distinctions both within cricket and outside it. He had many of the Renaissance Man qualities of C.B. Fry; but he was a shy person and often those who knew him well in one field were quite unaware of his achievements elsewhere. Perhaps his greatest cricketing feat was to cause the dismissals of both Hutton and Bradman for ducks in one week when playing for Cambridge University in May 1934. Against Yorkshire he ran out the young Hutton, who was making his first-class début and had pushed a ball to cover expecting to score his first run. The significance of this only became apparent with the years. But six days later he caused a sensation by clean bowling Bradman for his first-ever nought in England with a ball that went straight on and hit off stump. A large crowd at Fenner's was not entirely pleased with Davies.

The rest of his playing career, though a little anticlimactic, was still very successful, but conducted in the old-fashioned amateur way. He was a stylish and dashing right-hand batsman, mostly in the middle order (though he had a notably successful period as an opener for Kent in 1946), a slow off-break bowler capable of running through an innings and a brilliant cover-point. He had an outstanding school career at Tonbridge both inside and outside the classroom. He was a member of the cricket XI for four years, and captain in 1930, when he took 30 wickets and made 780 runs at 45.88; *Wisden* said he was rather too careless to be really brilliant.

Davies won a Classical Scholarship to St John's College, Cambridge and was all set for a Blue in 1931, but he sprained his ankle before the Lord's match and was forced to drop out. His place went to A.T. Ratcliffe, who scored 201. Davies played little in 1932 but finally earned recognition a year later, due to some steady bowling, and in 1934 he began to fulfil his batting promise with an outstanding 133 against Surrey at The Oval soon after his acts of *lèse majesté* at Fenner's. Davies then took eight wickets in the University match, including five for 43 in the first innings, which might have given Cambridge victory except that his captain, J.H. Human, did not bring him on until he had tried six other bowlers and the score was 318 for three. He also found time to take a first-class honours degree in classics – an unusual achievement for a cricket Blue, especially in that era – play rugby for Blackheath and Kent and win the Syriax Cup, the Rugby fives singles championship, three times. He played occasional matches for Kent before the war, and made 1,246 runs with three centuries as an opener in 1946, though he was a colonel at the time and had important War Office duties. His last first-class appearance, when he was almost 50, was for M.C.C. in 1961.

In 1939 Davies took a degree at the National Institute of Industrial Psychology and he became Chief Psychologist, Directorate for the Selection of Personnel, at the War Office. He later served at the United Nations. In 1952 he was appointed Secretary of the Cambridge University Appointments Board, and thereafter he became a father figure to generations of Cambridge cricketers. He was elected Treasurer of the Cambridge University Cricket Club in 1958 and for many years Davies and the groundsman Cyril Coote were the embodiment of the continuing traditions of Cambridge cricket. He was also Treasurer (1976–80) and

President (1985–86) of M.C.C. and was made an Honorary Vice-President in 1988. From 1969 to 1976 he was an executive director of the Bank of England. As late as 1990, he reported a couple of cricket matches from Fenner's for the *Daily Telegraph*. The sharpness of his mind was obvious to anyone who worked with him in committee, whatever the subject. His engaging laugh prevented his intelligence becoming too intimidating.

DELME-RADCLIFFE, ARTHUR HENRY, who died on June 30, 1950, was a native of South Tedworth, Hampshire. A member of the Sherborne XI before going to Oxford, he headed the school's batting averages in 1889. Subsequently he played for Hampshire and Berkshire. While batting for Hampshire against Somerset at Southampton in August 1889, he was concerned in a curious incident. Thinking he was out stumped, Delme-Radcliffe began to walk towards the pavilion, but the appeal had not been upheld. Then a fieldsman pulled up a stump and he was given out run out, but in the meantime the other umpire had called over, so the batsman continued his innings.

DEVERELL, SIR COLVILLE MONTGOMERY, who died on December 15, 1995, aged 89, played one first-class match, opening the batting with the playwright Samuel Beckett for Dublin University against Northamptonshire in 1926. Deverell made two and one. He was later Governor of the Windward Islands and then Mauritius, before becoming secretary-general of the International Planned Parenthood Federation.

DE ZOYSA, LUCIEN, who died on June 11, 1995, aged 78, represented Ceylon against various international touring teams and captured more than 500 wickets as a leg-spinner for Sinhalese Sports Club. He was also a successful cricket commentator, Shakespearean actor, writer and dramatist.

DOYLE, ANNIE GERTRUDE, died on July 4, 2005, aged 76. Nancy
Doyle was the *châtelaine* of the players' dining-room at Lord's for
many years until her retirement in 1996. Her lavish lunches – Mike
Brearley once asked, unsuccessfully, if she could limit the number of
courses to five – were legendary around a county circuit on which
the staple diet in most places at the time was salad, and she was
popular with generations of players. Nancy, who first worked at
Lord's as a waitress in 1961, was small yet volcanic, and some colleagues found her quick tongue hard to take. Steadfastly Irish to the
end, she was awarded an honorary MBE in 1994. She featured in
'An Alternative Five' cricket people of the year in *Wisden 1995*.

DOYLE, SIR ARTHUR CONAN, MD (Edin.), the well-known author,
born at Edinburgh on May 22, 1859, died at Crowborough, Sussex,
on July 7, 1930, aged 71. Although never a famous cricketer, he could
hit hard and bowl slows with a puzzling flight. For M.C.C. v.
Cambridgeshire at Lord's, in 1899, he took seven wickets for 61 runs,
and on the same ground two years later carried out his bat for 32
against Leicestershire, who had Woodcock, Geeson and King to
bowl for them. In *The Times* of October 27, 1915, he was the author
of an article on 'The Greatest of Cricketers: An Appreciation of Dr
Grace.' (It is said that Shacklock, the former Nottinghamshire
player, inspired him with the Christian name of his famous character, Sherlock Holmes, and that of the latter's brother Mycroft
was suggested by the Derbyshire cricketers.)

DRAKE, EDWARD JOSEPH, died on May 29, 1995, aged 82. Ted Drake
was an apprentice at the Southampton Gasworks before he made
his debut for Hampshire in 1931 and shared a vital stand of 86 with
Phil Mead against Glamorgan. He made 45 but never reached this
score again in the 15 further matches he played over the next six
years, first as an amateur and then as a professional. However, he
found greater glory in the winters, when Hampshire would have

paid him ten shillings a week, as one of the great centre-forwards of his era, first with Southampton and then with Arsenal, where he was transferred in 1934 for £5,000. He only won five England caps, but scored 42 goals in the 1934–35 season, an Arsenal record, and went on to manage Chelsea to the 1955 League Championship. He married the girl he met at the gasworks dance, not a detail associated with modern football stars of his magnitude.

DWYER, JOHN ELICIUS BENEDICT BERNARD PLACID QUIRK CARRINGTON (always referred to as E.B. Dwyer), died on October 19, 1912, at Crewe, where he had been engaged during the season. He was born on May 3, 1876, at Sydney (N.S.W.), where all his early cricket was played, first with the Redfern Wednesday C.C. and afterwards with Redfern. On P.F. Warner's suggestion he came to England in the spring of 1904, and early that year, whilst engaged temporarily at Lord's, came under the notice of C.B. Fry, who persuaded him to qualify for Sussex. His first match for the county was in 1906 and his last three seasons later, when, owing to lack of form, he dropped out of the side. In 1906 he took 96 wickets for 26.80 runs each, and in the following year 58 at an average cost of 27.65. Although having good pace, he was an unequal bowler, but deadly on his day. In 1906 he took nine wickets in an innings for 35 runs against Derbyshire, at Brighton, and 16 for 100 v. Notts. on the same ground – the first time for 80 years so many had been obtained by a bowler for Sussex in a match. In 1907, by taking six for 25 against the South Africans, he had a great deal to do with the Colonials being dismissed for 49, their smallest total during their tour. At times he hit hard and well, and at Brighton in 1906 scored 63 out of 82 in 50 minutes against Surrey. Dwyer was a great-grandson of Michael Dwyer, the Wicklow chieftain, who was one of the boldest leaders in the Irish insurrection of 1798. He held out for five years in the Wicklow mountains and was exiled in 1804 to Australia, where he died in 1826.

DYAL, REDVERS DUNDONALD, died on May 7, 1997, aged 96. King
Dyal was a lovable exhibitionist and one of the sights of Barbados.
He attended every major match at Kennington Oval for four
decades: a tall, slim, pipe-smoking figure wearing a brightly coloured
suit, which he would change at each interval before making a re-
entrance that would often attract more attention than the cricket.
He claimed never to have worked in his life. He died in poverty and
was buried at sea; former West Indies Cricket Board president
Peter Short delivered a eulogy.

E

EASTERBROOK, BASIL VIVIAN, who died on December 15, 1995, aged 75, was cricket and football writer for Kemsley (later Thomson Regional) Newspapers from 1950 to 1983 and thus covered all the major domestic matches for many of Britain's largest regional papers. He was a regular writer for *Wisden* and contributed an article every year from 1971 to 1980. Easterbrook was a much-loved member of the press corps with a puckish humour. He claimed that while covering a match from the old Lord's press box, he leaned out of the window to throw away his pencil shavings and the Nottinghamshire batsmen walked in, thinking it was the signal to declare. Once he phoned his office to dictate his copy, announced his name to the telephonist – Basil V. Easterbrook – to be greeted by the response 'What league is that in?' When he retired he wrote: 'The craft and practice of cricket writing was my personal window to the sky.'

EBERLE, VICTOR FULLER, who died in Bristol in 1974 aged about 90, claimed fame as the man who in 1899 dropped A.E.J. Collins when he had scored 20. It was in the House Match at Clifton College in which Collins went on to score 628 not out!

ECKERSLEY, LIEUT. PETER THORP, RNVR, MP, died on August 13, 1940, at the age of 36, as the outcome of an accident when flying. Known as the 'cricketer-airman', he often flew his own plane to matches. In 1928, when prospective candidate for the Newton division of Lancashire, he announced the compulsion of deciding between politics and cricket and that he chose cricket. Experience at Rugby and Cambridge University, where he did not get his Blue, equipped

Eckersley so well in batting and fielding that after one season in the XI he was appointed captain of the Lancashire County Club when only 24. This difficult position, with little amateur companionship, he held with honour for six years and led his side to the Championship in 1934.

In the seasons 1923 to 1936 Eckersley often played well when his side were badly placed, and he scored 5,730 runs, including a very good century against Gloucestershire at Bristol. A first-rate fields-man, he set his team a splendid example, notably at times when some slackness was apparent. Still, he retained a liking for politics and, reversing his previous decision, he contested the Leigh Division in 1931 before he achieved his ambition by becoming Unionist Member of Parliament for the Exchange Division of Manchester in 1935. He consequently resigned the captaincy of Lancashire, but his restless nature, known so well to intimate friends, influenced him to join the Air Arm of the RNVR when war broke out. Despite indifferent health he was always keen for duty until his strength became overtaxed.

EDWARD VII, H.M. KING, died at Buckingham Palace on May 6, 1910. As a small boy he received tuition at Windsor from F. Bell, of Cambridge, but it cannot be said that he ever showed much aptitude for the game. He played occasionally during his Oxford days, however, and, while he was staying at Madingley Hall, a special wicket was reserved for his use at Fenner's. He showed his interest in the game in many ways. When funds were being col-lected to pay off the pavilion debt at Fenner's, he contributed £10, at the same time promising to make up any amount required at the end of the term, and during one of the critical moments in the history of the M.C.C. was the largest contributor to the fund raised to pay for the freehold of Lord's. Furthermore, as Duke of Cornwall his late Majesty was for many years landlord of The Oval, and in several ways he showed his interest in the Surrey

County C.C. His Majesty was born at Buckingham Palace on November 9, 1841, and was therefore in his 69th year at the time of his death.

ELIGON, DONALD, died at Port of Spain, Trinidad, on June 4, 1937, aged 28. After playing for Shannon Cricket Club he joined the Trinidad inter-colonial team in 1934 and quickly became one of the outstanding bowlers in West Indies. Last season he took seven wickets for 63 runs in the second innings against British Guiana, and five for 39 against Grenada. His death was due to blood poisoning caused by a nail in his cricket boot.

EVANS, ALFRED JOHN, who died in London on September 18, 1959, aged 71, was a fine all-round sportsman. Educated at Winchester, where his father, A.H. Evans, a former Oxford cricket Blue and captain, was a master, he won both the schools racquets and the golf in 1905 and the two succeeding years, and played at Lord's for three years. Going up to Oxford he won his cricket Blue as a Freshman in 1909, scoring 79 and 46. He also played against Cambridge in the three following seasons, doing good work as a hard-driving batsman and medium-paced bowler. He led the side in 1911. In 1910 he represented his University at racquets and in 1909 and 1910 at golf. He played cricket for Hampshire in 1911 and, after serving with distinction in the Royal Flying Corps during the First World War, when he earned fame for his escapes from enemy prison-camps, he assisted Kent and M.C.C. In 1921, on the strength of an innings of 69 not out for M.C.C. against the Australians, he was chosen for England in the Test match at Lord's, but was not a success.

EVANS, GWYNFOR, who died on April 21, 2005, aged 92, was Plaid Cymru's first Westminster MP, representing Carmarthen from 1966 to 1970 and again from 1974 to 1979. He was best known for

threatening to starve himself to death to pressurise the government into conceding a Welsh-language TV station; the threat was enough to secure victory. In his youth he had played cricket for Glamorgan Schools, and he retained his love of the game.

EVERARD, SIR WILLIAM LINDSAY, DL, JP, died at Torquay on March 11, 1949, aged 57. Harrow XI 1908. Played twice for Leicestershire. Hon. Secretary of Leicestershire Gentlemen's Club 1914–35. President of County Club 1936 and 1939; member of the M.C.C. Committee 1938–45. One of the pioneers of private flying at his own aerodrome near his Leicestershire home, Ratcliffe Hall. Vice-President and former Chairman of Royal Aero Club, M.P. for Melton 1924–45. Knighted 1939.

EVERY, TREVOR, who died at Newport on January 20, 1990, just after his 80th birthday, had to contend with a tragedy which brought to an abrupt end his career with Glamorgan as a wicket-keeper-batsman. At the pre-season nets in 1934, he found to his dismay that he was unable to pick up properly the flight of the ball. However, he started the opening match, against Kent at Cardiff, keeping wickets as usual: the scorecard shows that he must have asked for relief about halfway through Kent's first innings; and batting at No. 10 he was bowled by Freeman for 0. He was never to step on to a cricket field again. Within a day or two a specialist pronounced his optic nerve to be deteriorating so rapidly that he would soon be totally blind. Glamorgan made a moving appeal on his behalf, and more than £1,000 was raised to help him adjust to a very different way of life.

Every, who was born at Llanelli, was playing for the local club when he was spotted by some Glamorgan professionals, who recommended him for a trial with the county. In 1929 he played in 19 matches, sharing the wicket-keeping duties with two other young professionals, and in 1930 he trained on into a first-rate keeper. He completed 47 dismissals, a total he equalled in 1932. The highlight of his season in 1933 was the day he and Dai Davies, both local boys, made 75 and 70 respectively at Llanelli in a Championship match. They were cheered to the echo by a large and enthusiastic crowd. Then darkness fell. It is clear that, under the captaincy of M.J. Turnbull, a cricketer of high promise, lively personality, and good humour was developing along a path which might have taken him to the top. In his short career he disposed of 179 batsmen, of whom 70 were stumped, and scored 2,518 runs for an average of 16.35. After his loss of sight, he was trained in Cardiff as a stenographer by the Royal National Institute for the Blind, for whom he worked for many years. Nor did he ever lose touch with the game which had promised him so much.

EWART, GAVIN BUCHANAN, who died on October 23, 1995, aged 79, was a well-known poet and a lifelong cricket enthusiast. He produced many poems on cricket, penning *A Pindaric Ode* on the 1981 Headingley Test as well as shorter lyrics of wry nostalgia and a squib on the radio commentary team. His most substantial piece, *The Sadness of Cricket*, was a poignant elegy for the players of the Golden Age:

> We'd one at Wellington, that A.E. Relf,
> Who'd bowled for England – long since on the shelf –
> In 1937 stalled and shot himself.
> Remembered bowling in the nets,
> A little irritable (I thought – but one forgets),
> Doling out stumps to junior games, like doubtful debts,
> From the pavilion's mean back door.

F

FABER, CANON ARTHUR HENRY, of the Winchester XI of 1847 and 1848, was born in India on February 29, 1832, and died at Doncaster, on November 29, 1910. In his four Public School matches he scored 54 runs in eight innings, took 10 wickets, and on every occasion was on the beaten side. He did not obtain his Blue at Oxford, although he was a far better batsman than his scores against Eton and Harrow would lead one to suppose. *Scores and Biographies* described Canon Faber as 'A most excellent batsman,' and added that he played frequently under the name of St Fabian.

FARGUS, THE REV. ARCHIBALD HUGH CONWAY, who went down in the *Monmouth*, Admiral Cradock's flagship, in the action in the Pacific on November 1, 1914, was born at Clifton, Bristol, on December 15, 1878, and was educated at Clifton, Haileybury and Cambridge. He appeared for Cambridge in the drawn games with Oxford in 1900 and 1901, in which he made 8 and 17 not out and obtained six wickets for 260 runs. He assisted Gloucestershire in 1900 and 1901 and Devonshire in 1904, and had been a member of the M.C.C. since 1901. He was described as a stout hitter, a good hammer and tongs bowler, and a hard-working field. Since 1907 he had been a Chaplain in the Royal Navy, and in 1913 was appointed Vicar of Askham Richard, York. At the beginning of the War he became temporary Acting-Chaplain to the *Monmouth*.*

* In fact, Fargus had missed a train and failed to rejoin the *Monmouth*. He survived until 1963.

FENNER, F.P.'s death, on May 22, 1896, destroyed one of the few remaining links between the cricket of the present day and the generation of Mynn and Fuller Pilch. Born at Cambridge on March 1, 1811, Mr Fenner had reached a ripe old age. In his day he was a capital cricketer, taking his part with no little distinction in big matches, but his fame rests not so much upon what he did in the field, as on the fact that he laid out the beautiful ground at Cambridge, which, though now the property of the University, is nearly always spoken of by old cricketers as Fenner's. The ground was opened in 1846, and is still, after 50 years' play, one of the best in the world. Mr Fenner played his first match at Lord's in 1832, appearing for the Cambridge Town Club against the M.C.C. On that occasion Fuller Pilch played for the Cambridge Club as a given man and with scores of 50 and not out 41, won the match.

FIELD, 2ND LIEUT. OLIVER (DURHAM LIGHT INFANTRY), was killed in action in France on July 18, 1915, aged 42. A steady batsman and good field, he was in the Clifton College XI in 1890, when he scored 113 runs with an average of 14.12. Proceeding to Oxford, he played for Trinity in 1892 and 1893, averaging 29.00 in the former year and 27.50 in the latter. He was a direct descendant of Oliver Cromwell.

FILLISTON, JOSEPH W., who died in hospital on October 25, 1964, aged 102, five days after being knocked down by a motor-scooter, acted as umpire to the B.C.C. Cricket Club for many years. Old Joe stood in the Old England v. Lord's Taverners match at Lord's when over 100. In his younger days he played cricket with Dr W.G. Grace and he helped Gentlemen of Kent defeat the Philadelphians by six wickets at Town Mailing in 1889. He also played as a professional in the Staffordshire League. He liked to tell of the occasion when he gave W.G. out leg-before in a London County game at the Crystal Palace. The Doctor, he said, refused to leave the crease and, as nobody had the courage to contradict him, he continued his innings.

FISON, THOMAS ARTHUR, a well-known figure in Metropolitan cricket
circles about a quarter of a century ago, died at Hampstead, on April
14, 1911. As captain of the Hendon C.C. against Highgate School in
August, 1879, he scored 264 not out in three hours and a half, hitting
a seven, two fives, nine fours, 23 threes, and 40 twos. All the hits were
run out, and in the score-sheet it was recorded that he retired to
catch a train for the Continent. In a match between the same sides at
Hendon in 1884 he made 201. Mr Fison was 6ft. 2ins. in height, and
was a good wicket-keeper. He was born at Romsey, in Hampshire,
on October 7, 1853, and was educated at Mill Hill School.

FORSTER, LORD, OF LEPE, PC, GCMG, died on January 15, 1936, when
nearly 70 years of age. During three years in the Eton XI H.W.
Forster did not meet with much success in the important school
matches but he scored, in irreproachable style, mainly by off-drives
and cuts, 60 not out for Oxford against Cambridge in 1887.
Essentially a fast-wicket batsman, he often got out disappointingly
after rain, but on true turf he showed most attractive stroke play. He
was a member of the Hampshire XI for several seasons until 1895,
mostly under F.E. Lacey.

  In 1919, before being raised to the Peerage, he became President of
M.C.C., his former Hampshire Captain then being Secretary at
Lord's. As Governor-General of Australia, Lord Forster took special
interest in cricket in the Commonwealth and entertained the M.C.C.
touring teams. In 1925, during the third Test match at Adelaide, when
Arthur Gilligan's team lost the rubber, he unveiled a portrait of
George Giffen, who came to England in 1882, helped Australia to
victory by seven runs in The Ashes match, and paid several other
visits. Lord Forster, who was born on January 31, 1866, stood over six
feet high and, with powerful physique, had a commanding figure.

FOWLER, CAPT. ROBERT ST LEGER, MC, born on April 7, 1891, died at
Rahinston, Enfield, County Meath, on June 13, 1925, aged 34.

Owing to his profession, he was not very well-known to the general cricket public, but he was the hero of a match which may, without exaggeration, be described as the most extraordinary ever played.

The story of the Eton and Harrow match in 1910 has been told over and over again, but it can never grow stale. No victory in a match of widespread interest was ever snatched in such a marvellous way. As captain of the Eton XI, Fowler – it was his third year in the big match – found his side for about a day and a half overwhelmed. On the first day Harrow scored 232, and Eton, before bad light caused stumps to be drawn, lost five wickets for 40 runs. This was bad enough, but worse was to come. Eton's innings ended on the Saturday morning for 67, and in the follow-on five wickets were lost for 65. Fowler, scoring 64, played splendidly and received valuable help, but, in spite of all his efforts, the game reached a point at which the odds on Harrow could not have been named. With one wicket to fall Eton were only four runs ahead. But the Hon. J.N. Manners – killed in the War in 1914 – hit so fearlessly and had such a cool-headed partner in Lister-Kaye that the last wicket put on 50 runs. Honour was in a measure saved, no one imagined that Harrow would fail to get the 55 runs required. Then came the crowning sensation. Fowler bowled his off-breaks with such deadly accuracy that he took eight wickets – five of them bowled down – and won the match for Eton by nine runs.

No one who was at Lord's on that eventful Saturday evening will ever forget the scene at the finish. Old Harrovians, bearing their sorrow with as much fortitude as could have been expected, said sadly that a grievous blunder had been committed in putting the heavy roller on the rather soft pitch, and there was a good deal in their contention. Still, nothing could detract from Fowler's achievement. Something heroic was demanded of him, and he rose to the height of his opportunity. From one point of view it was a pity he went into the Army. In Oxford or Cambridge cricket he would assuredly have played a great part. In the First World War he served as Captain in the 17th Lancers and gained the Military Cross.

FOWLES, JOHN ROBERT, who died on November 5, 2005, aged 79, was a novelist whose work included *The Magus* and *The French Lieutenant's Woman*. Cricket remained a lifelong interest from the time Fowles learned the game from the Essex captain, Denys Wilcox, at Alleyn Court prep school in Westcliff-on-Sea. He and Trevor Bailey used to cycle there together. As a fast bowler, Fowles took plenty of wickets for Bedford School, which he captained in 1944, and had a trial for Essex. His off-cutter remained a source of pride – though demonstrations of how he achieved this were lost on American film directors. While watching England nervily bat to victory over the West Indies at Lord's in 2000, he was joined in his living room in Lyme Regis by a stranger asking the score. When Fowles told him, his visitor sat down and watched with him until Dominic Cork had hit the winning runs. Only when he subsequently asked how much Fowles charged for bed and breakfast, did both men realise that the stranger had walked uninvited into the wrong house.

G

GAINFORD, LORD, who died at Headlam Hall, near Darlington, on February 15, 1943, aged 83, captained Durham County Club from 1886 to 1891, and continued playing cricket until he was 74, when, as he wrote to Mr Bulmer, secretary of Durham County C.C., 'Inability to take a quick run forced me to give up the game.' His last innings was nine not out. Joseph Albert Pease, known as Jack, joined the county club on its formation in 1882 and was the oldest member. He played for the county until 1892, having a batting average of nearly 19, and he kept wicket. In 1878 he went to Cambridge, captained Trinity College cricket XI, played in the polo team, was master of the drag hounds, and sometimes played rugby for the University without getting his Blue. 'One of the proudest moments of my life,' he used to relate, 'was when I took a catch in the outfield off W.G. Grace, who shook me by the hand.' That was in a match for M.C.C., of which he was a member for many years.

During 34 years in the House of Commons he became Postmaster-General, President of the Board of Education, Chancellor of the Duchy of Lancaster, and Chief Liberal Whip. He was raised to the Peerage in 1916 and took an active part in House of Lords debates. Shortly before his death he recalled an occasion in the Commons some 50 years ago when a fray arose over the Home Rule for Ireland Bill, and he used the rugby tackle to keep Dr Tanner out of the maul until John Burns separated the combatants.

GALE, FREDERICK – well known to thousands of cricketers under his nom de plume of 'The Old Buffer' – died on April 24, 1904, in the Charterhouse. Born in 1823, he had lived to a ripe old age. He was in the Winchester XI in 1841, and appeared at Lord's that year against both Harrow and Eton. Winchester suffered a single-innings defeat at the hands of Harrow, but beat Eton by 109 runs. The victory was one to be proud of, as the Eton team included Emilius Bayley, Walter Marcon, George Yonge, and Harvey Fellows. Mr Gale did not win fame as a player, but no one loved cricket more than he did, or supported it more keenly. He kept up his enthusiasm to the end, and even so recently as the season of 1903 he was to be seen at The Oval – bent in figure, but still full of vivacity.

As a writer on the game he was prolific, several books and numberless magazine and newspaper articles coming from his pen. He lived for a good many years at Mitcham, and in those days took the liveliest interest in young Surrey players, delighting in the triumphs of Jupp, Tom Humphrey, and, a little later, Richard Humphrey. A special protegé of his was George Jones, who bowled for Surrey more than 20 years ago, when the county's fortunes were at a low ebb. Mr Gale had a high ideal of the way in which cricket should be played, and in his various writings always insisted on the necessity of good fielding. His particular aversion was the batsman who played for his average rather than for his side. Like many old men, he had an abiding regard for the heroes of his youth, and nothing pleased him better, when he found a congenial listener, than to talk about Fuller Pilch, Hillyer, and Felix. Still, he could be just as enthusiastic when discussing the batting of W.G. Grace and the bowling of Alfred Shaw. He enjoyed the friendship of John Ruskin, and took the famous writer to The Oval in 1882 to see the Australians.

GANDAR-DOWER, KENNETH CECIL, was lost at sea through Japanese action in February, 1944, at the age of 36. He played for Harrow against Winchester in 1927, but not in the Eton match. At Cambridge he did well in the Freshmen's match and was a Crusader, but his time was mainly given up to tennis, at which he captained the University team. One of the most versatile players of games of any period, he was amateur squash champion in 1938, won amateur championships at fives, and played lawn tennis for Great Britain. In all, he represented Cambridge at six forms of sport: tennis, lawn tennis, Rugby fives, Eton fives, squash racquets and billiards. In fact, time hardly sufficed for their rival calls. He probably created a record when he played simultaneously in the Freshmen's match and Freshmen's tournament, with the connivance of the tennis but not the cricket authorities; he disappeared to play off a round during the early part of his side's innings, with relays of cyclist friends to keep him informed as to the fall of wickets! He flew a private aeroplane to India. In spite of other demands he continued to find time for cricket, making some 10 appearances for the Frogs each season almost to the outbreak of war, and got many runs and wickets.

Famous as a big game shot, and extensive traveller, he introduced a team of cheetahs from the Kenyan jungle to London and on greyhound tracks they set up speed records. A writer of articles and books, he acted as a War Correspondent in various theatres of operations up to the time of his death.

GARLAND-WELLS, HERBERT MONTANDON, died on May 28, 1993, aged 85. Monty Garland-Wells was one of the leading amateur characters of the immediate pre-war period. Educated at St Paul's, he scored 64 not out and 70 for Oxford in the Varsity match in 1928, the year he made his debut for Surrey. He was a sporting all-rounder – he kept goal for the England amateur football team – and a cricketing one. As a middle-order batsman, his batting never again touched the heights it did at University; nevertheless he, Errol Holmes and Freddie Brown were referred to at Surrey as the Biff-Bang Boys. He also bowled medium-pace cutters good enough to bowl Bradman for 32 in May 1930 when he was striving for his 1,000. Garland-Wells took over the Surrey captaincy in 1939 and captained the team as he played, with a touch of unorthodoxy in the tradition of Percy Fender; he was also very popular with the professionals without a hint of amateur aloofness. It promised to be a successful as well as a happy reign; however, the war came and commitments as a solicitor prevented him carrying on in 1946. Thereafter, he concentrated on golf and bowls. In the war his name was informally used as a code word in North Africa: Garland-Wells = Monty = Montgomery. This was more impenetrable to the Germans than the most complicated cipher.

GEORGE TUBOW II, KING OF TONGA. The last of the independent kings in the Pacific. Died April 1918, aged 46. Very fond of cricket, gaining his love of the game while at school in Auckland. His subjects became so devoted to the game that it was necessary to prohibit it on six days of the week in order to avert famine, the plantations being entirely neglected for the cricket field.

GIBSON, GEORGE, a native of Jamaica, died at Carlton, Melbourne, on September 5, 1910, aged 83. His first appearance in a match of note was for Victoria v. New South Wales, on the Melbourne ground, in December, 1865, and his highest innings in a first-class game 41 – against the same colony in March, 1872 – for playing which, he was presented with a bat made from a willow-tree grown in his own garden. In addition to being a capable batsman, he was a good wicket-keeper.

GEORGE V, H.M. KING, died at Sandringham on January 20, 1936. As Duke of Cornwall, when Prince of Wales, His Majesty was ground landlord of Kennington Oval, and remained Patron of the Surrey club until his death. King George was also Patron of M.C.C., and the book Lord's and The M.C.C. by Lord Harris and F. S. Ashley-Cooper, published in 1914, was dedicated by gracious permission to His Majesty.

GEORGE VI, H.M. KING, died at Sandringham on February 6, 1952. He was Patron of the Marylebone, Surrey and Lancashire clubs. When Prince Albert he performed the hat-trick on the private ground on the slopes below Windsor Castle, where the sons and grandsons of Edward VII used to play regularly. A left-handed batsman and bowler, the King bowled King Edward VII, King George V and the present Duke of Windsor in three consecutive balls, thus proving himself the best Royal cricketer since Frederick, Prince of Wales, in 1751, took a keen interest in the game. The ball is now mounted in the mess-room of the Royal Naval College, Dartmouth.

King George VI, like his father, often went to Lord's when Commonwealth teams were playing there, and invariably the players and umpires were presented to His Majesty in front of the pavilion. He entertained the 1948 Australian team at Balmoral, and in his 1949 New Year's Honours Donald Bradman, the captain, received a Knighthood.

GILLINGHAM, REV. GEORGE WILLIAM, who died on June 11, 1953, after a ministry of 52 years, played cricket for Gentlemen of Worcestershire before the First World War. Though never attaining first-class standards, he was a great cricket enthusiast who did much good work for Worcestershire. When becoming Rector of St Martin's, Worcester, he revived and managed the Worcestershire Club and Ground matches, and in 1923 he organised a bazaar which realised £2,300 for the County Club. From 1929 he acted for some seasons as honorary secretary to Worcestershire in order that the secretary, C.F. Walters, could play for the county. During this period when, during the winter the River Severn flooded the county ground at Worcester, Gillingham swam across the ground to gain access to the pavilion and returned with the account books.

He was author of *The Cardinal's Treasure*, a romance of the Elizabethan age, part of the proceeds from which he devoted to

the Worcestershire C.C.C. and the R.S.P.C.A. When Vicar of St Mark's, Coventry, he was for four years tenant of a condemned public house, The Barley Mow, which he transformed into a Hooligans' Club where boxing and Bible classes went hand-in-hand.

GOAD, FRANCIS EDWARD, who died at Godstone, Surrey, on May 19, 1951, aged 82, played for Eton in 1888 when, thanks to the all-round work of F.S. Jackson and R.B. Hoare, nephew of Sir Samuel Hoare, Harrow won by 156 runs. In the Eton second innings of 52, Goad scored 22. Jackson scored 21 and 59 and took five wickets for 28. Before the match commenced, his father promised him a sovereign for every wicket he took and a shilling for every run he made. Congratulated afterwards upon his efforts, Jackson is said to have replied: 'I don't care so much for myself, but it'll give the guv'nor such a lift!' Goad was for many years principal fur auctioneer for the Hudson Bay Company.

GORDON, SIR HOME SETON CHARLES MONTAGU, 12TH BARONET GORDON OF EMBO, SUTHERLANDSHIRE, who died suddenly at his home at Rottingdean on September 9, 1956, aged 84, was celebrated as a cricket historian. Always immaculately dressed and wearing a red carnation, he was known on grounds all over the country. He began a journalistic career immediately he left Eton in 1887 and at one time was the sole proprietor of the publishing house of Williams & Norgate Ltd. He used to say that the ideal publisher was the man who builds upon three rocks – the Public, the Press and the Bookseller.

Among his books on cricket were *Cricket Form at a Glance*, *A Biography of W.G. Grace*, *Background of Cricket*, and *A History of Sussex Cricket*; he did much work in connection with annuals for county clubs and contributed to the *Encyclopaedia Britannica*. As a young man he played for M.C.C. amateur sides, but never took part in first-class cricket, though, for his services to Sussex, he was awarded a county cap – an old one belonging to A.E.R. Gilligan.

His memory of the game went back to 1878 when, not seven years old, he was taken to the Gentlemen of England v. Australians match at Prince's. He first went to Lord's on Whit Monday, 1880, being presented to W.G. Grace. In that season he watched the first England v. Australia Test match at The Oval and saw Alfred Lyttelton keep wicket for Middlesex against Gloucestershire at Clifton in a hard straw hat. During his long life he attended no fewer than 70 Oxford v. Cambridge games.

He was on terms of intimate friendship with such great figures of the past as K.S. Ranjitsinhji, with whom he drove in a silver coach to the Delhi Durbar, Lord Hawke and Lord Harris. He was President of the London Club Cricketers' Conference in 1917–18; chairman of the Sports Conference in 1919, and had held practically every honorary position for Sussex, becoming President in 1948. He was also captain of the Rye Golf Club. He succeeded his father in the Baronetcy in 1906, but, as there were no children of either of his two marriages, the title, created by King Charles I in 1631, becomes extinct.

GREEN, BERNARD, died on June 22, 1998, aged 70. Benny Green was a jazz musician, broadcaster, writer and wit who had the rare ability to make unexpected connections between his various enthusiasms, and delighted millions of people in the process. Among those enthusiasms were cricket – he grew up watching Compton at Lord's – and, most specifically, *Wisden*, which he regarded as a work of glorious social history. He reviewed the Almanack one year in *The Spectator*, and suggested there ought to be an anthology. There was only one candidate for the job.

In 1979 he began work, reading the entire canon cover-to-cover before slimming down the first 119 editions into four (chunky) volumes, brought alive by Green's eye for telling and quirky detail.

This turned into a cottage industry: spin-offs included *The Wisden Book of Obituaries* (1986), *The Wisden Papers* (1989) and *The Concise Wisden* (1990), originally published two years earlier especially for Marks & Spencer, a very Greenish connection itself. His various introductions are mini-classics.

He also published a number of other cricket books, including a notably eclectic non-*Wisden* anthology, *The Cricket Addict's Archive* (later retitled *Benny Green's Cricket Archive*). He talked about everything with an auto-didact's zest, and in an unchanging Cockney accent. 'The effect,' wrote Dave Gelly in the *Observer*, 'was as though a particularly grumpy taxi-driver had started quoting Dr Johnson while sorting out your change.'

GREGORY, ARTHUR H., born at Sydney on July 7, 1861, died at Chatswood, Sydney, on August 17, 1929, aged 68. Returning from the funeral of S.E. Gregory he fell from a tramcar, and blood-poisoning supervened as a result of injuries to his arm. He was a member of the most famous of Australian cricket families, and, although perhaps better known as a graceful and well-informed writer on the game, was a sound batsman, a good field and a fair leg-break bowler and had himself appeared for New South Wales. He was younger brother of E.J., D.W., and C.S. Gregory, and uncle of S.E., C.W. and J.M.

GROVES, GEORGE JASPER, died on February 18, 1941, as the result of a wound suffered through enemy action when at Newmarket on duty as a racing journalist. Born on October 19, 1868, in Nottingham, where his Yorkshire parents were on a visit, he had a county quali-fication which was discovered by a friend watching him make many runs for the Richmond club, and a recommendation obtained for him a trial when 30 years of age in the 1899 August Bank Holiday match at The Oval.

At that time he ran a sports reporting business, founded by his father, and he was well-known in the Press world. I was one of several in the Press box anxious for his success, and we were delighted at the way he overcame the ordeal of facing Lockwood, Richardson, Hayward, Brockwell and Lees before a 20,000 crowd. He said to me afterwards, 'Tom Richardson gave me a short one on the leg side and the four, that was a gift, quietened my nerves.' He made 42, helping A.O. Jones in a stand that stopped a collapse of Notts.

Against Middlesex at Trent Bridge his 51, the highest score in the Notts second innings, could not stave off defeat by 10 wickets, brought about mainly by the all-round play of C.M. Wells, who batted grandly for 244 and took nine wickets for 111 runs with his slows. His highest innings in County Cricket, 56 not out, after a grand 137 by William Gunn, helped towards a dramatic victory over Kent. Very consistent, Groves averaged 23.36 during two seasons in county matches, but journalistic duties compelled him to give up first-class cricket. A small man of rather light build, Groves used the hook stroke and cut well. He fielded very smartly, usually at third man.

He learned games at school in Sheffield, and played Association football for that city against London – a great match for amateurs. He was a useful member of Sheffield United before his family settled in London. Then he captained Woolwich Arsenal in the old days at Plumstead. A full-back at one time, and then centre-half, he was a strong skilful player, and I enjoyed many games in his company for mid-week amateur teams. Good at billiards, he often acted as referee in professional matches.

H

HALFYARD, DAVID JOHN, who died suddenly on August 23, 1996, aged 65, had a remarkable, indeed eccentric, career which was supposed to have ended after a serious road accident in 1962. But he returned to the first-class game six years later and was still taking wickets for Tiverton Heathcoat in the Devon Premier League a few weeks before he died. Dave Halfyard came to prominence as a tireless seamer for Kent in the late 1950s, and took 135 wickets in 1958. After his accident he kept trying to make a comeback, but failed, and in 1967 went on to the first-class umpires' list.

However, Nottinghamshire saw him bowling in the nets – in itself not normal practice for an umpire – and decided to sign him, although almost the entire committee had to watch him for two hours before they were convinced of his fitness. He thus became perhaps the only umpire to retire and return to playing. Bowling more sedately but even more craftily than he did for Kent, he spent three productive years at Nottinghamshire, bringing his total of first-class wickets to 963 before finally leaving the first-class game in 1970. Even while with Nottinghamshire he would slip away on his days off to bowl leg-breaks for club sides. Over the next 12 years he had spells as professional with Durham, Northumberland and Cornwall and had another period as an umpire. While with Cornwall, he took all 16 Devon wickets to fall in a match at Penzance.

Halfyard's zest for displaying the tricks of his trade before audiences others might have thought unworthy made him in that sense comparable to Sydney Barnes. His pride and joy was a camper van with almost 400,000 miles on the clock; his cricket had the same improbable durability.

HARBOTTLE, BRIG. MICHAEL NEALE, OBE, who died on May 1, 1997, aged 80, played one innings in his only first-class match, and scored 156, for the Army against Oxford University at Camberley in 1938. Harbottle emerged as a talented left-handed batsman at Marlborough. He was rejected by the Navy because of bunions, but these did not bother the Army and he became captain of the Sandhurst XI. In the 1960s he became chief of staff for the UN peace-keeping force in Cyprus and was later an organiser of Generals for Peace and Disarmament.

HARDING, HIS HONOUR W. ROWE, who died on February 10, 1991, aged 89, was chairman of Glamorgan from 1959 to 1976 and president of the club from 1979 until the time of his death. He had taken over as chairman following a period of internal dispute which led to the resignation of the previous chairman, Colonel J.M. Bevan, and ten of his committee. The old committee had tried to dispense with the services of Glamorgan's captain/secretary, Wilf Wooller, as secretary on a permanent basis, and when the matter was put to the members in a referendum, the answer was a decisive vote of no confidence in the committee. It was greatly due to Harding's good sense that the affair was soon largely forgotten. A well-known figure in South Wales legal circles, he was a circuit judge for 22 years. In the 1920s he played 17 times for Wales as a wing three-quarter and was a member of the 1924 British Lions in South Africa.

HARDY, PRIVATE FREDERICK PERCY (County of London Yeomanry), born at Blandford on June 26, 1881, was found dead on the floor of a lavatory at King's Cross station (G.N.R.) on March 9, 1916. His throat was cut and a blood-stained knife was by his side. He was on The Oval ground-staff in 1900 and 1901 and began to appear for Somerset in 1903. In consecutive innings for the Surrey Colts in 1901 he made 141 v. Wandsworth and 144 not out v. Mitcham Wanderers. In 1910 he played two excellent innings at Taunton, making 91 v.

Kent and 79 v. Surrey. He was a left-handed batsman and a useful right-handed medium-paced change bowler.

HARRIS, LIEUT.-COL. FRANK, who died at Tunbridge Wells on July 2, 1957, aged 91, was for 35 years captain of Southborough C.C., for whom he first played when 16. In his younger days an enthusiastic runner, he walked from Bidborough to London on his 70th birthday because his father did the same thing and had told him that he would not be able to do so when he was 70. The journey occupied him just over 13 hours. He served in the Royal Engineers during the First World War, being Mentioned in Dispatches.

HASEEB-UL-HASAN, who was murdered by an unknown gunman at Joharabad, Pakistan on April 18, 1990, aged 25, had played in 32 first-class matches for Karachi and Karachi Blues since 1984–85. Only a month earlier, bowling left-arm medium-pace, he had taken five for 66, career-best figures, against Karachi Whites in the final of the Patron's Trophy. In all he took 59 wickets at 31.50 apiece, while his left-hand batting produced 1,365 runs for an average of 31.02.

HEMINGWAY, GEORGE EDWARD, a brother of Messrs. W.M.G. and R.E. Hemingway, died at Rangoon on March 11, 1907. He was born at Macclesfield in 1872, was in the Uppingham XI in 1888, and in 1898 appeared for Gloucestershire against Yorkshire, at Sheffield. He was a free batsman and in the field generally stood mid-off or cover-point, but business and weak sight handicapped his play considerably. On one occasion, when playing a single-wicket match against his two brothers, he hit the ball into a bed of nettles; the fieldsmen quarrelled as to who should recover it, and during the argument the batsman ran about 250.

HILL, H. JOHN, father of the well-known Australian cricketing brotherhood which included Clement Hill, died in Adelaide on

September 18, 1926. A good player in his day, he will be remembered chiefly for having been the first batsman to play a three-figure innings on the Adelaide Oval – 102 not out for North Adelaide v. Kent C.C. on January 26, 1878. A trustee of the South Australian Cricket Association for many years and vice-president of that body since 1893, Mr Hill was also a famous whip and in 1874 he drove W.G. Grace's team to Kadina in one of his four-in-hands. Born in Adelaide on March 16, 1847, he was, at the time of his death, in his 80th year.

HODGES, EDWARD, a nephew of the famous John Willes, was born at Bellringham, Sutton Valence, on February 11, 1819 and died at Southsea on February 20, 1907. His name will be found in the match between the Gentlemen of Kent and I Zingari at Canterbury in 1853. It was his mother who gave her brother, Mr John Willes, the idea of round-armed bowling by throwing to him in practice in a barn at Fonford, near Canterbury.

HOLMES, GROUP CAPT. ALBERT JOHN, AFC AND BAR, died suddenly at his home at Burwash after a heart attack on May 21, 1950. Born at Thornton Heath, Surrey, on June 30, 1899, he was a member of the Test Match Selection Committee in 1939, became Chairman for the first four seasons following the War, and was appointed for 1950, but resigned through ill-health upon the advice of his doctor. Generally known among cricketers as Jack, he was educated at Repton, where he did well as a batsman. After service in the First World War, in the Royal Field Artillery and then with the Royal Flying Corps, he made his first appearance for Sussex in 1923, scoring over 1,000 runs, but in 1925 he rejoined the Royal Air Force, and not until 1935, when he transferred to the Reserve, was he able to play again for the county.

Then, when A. Melville resigned the position before returning to South Africa, Holmes took over the Sussex captaincy, which he held till the outbreak of the Second World War, when he returned to the R.A.F. In 1940, when a Wing Commander, he was awarded the Air Force Cross and received a Bar to the decoration in 1942. His genial personality made him very popular and contributed largely to his success as manager of the M.C.C. team which toured South Africa in 1938–39. He was a pioneer of mink farming in England.

HOME OF THE HIRSEL, THE BARON, KT, PC, who died at his home on October 9, 1995, aged 92, was the only British prime minister to have played first-class cricket. As Lord Dunglass, he was a useful member of the Eton XI. In the rain-affected Eton-Harrow match of 1922 he scored 66, despite being hindered by a saturated outfield, and then took four for 37 with his medium-paced out-swingers. He played ten first-class matches for six different teams: Middlesex, Oxford University, H.D.G. Leveson Gower's XI, M.C.C. (with whom he toured South America under Pelham Warner), Free Foresters and Harlequins. His two games for Middlesex were in 1924 and 1925, both against Oxford University while he was actually an Oxford undergraduate; he did not represent the university until the following year.

His cricket was gradually overtaken by politics, and he entered the Commons in 1931. After he succeeded to his father's title and became the 14th Earl of Home, he rose to be foreign secretary and then prime minister, when he emerged as a totally unexpected compromise choice as Harold Macmillan's successor. After renouncing his title (and becoming Sir Alec Douglas-Home until he returned to the Lords as a life peer) he remained in Downing Street for a year until the 1964 election.

Despite all his honours, Alec Home never made an enemy and was much valued, in cricket as in politics, for his quiet charm and sagacity. He was president of M.C.C. in 1966 and an important behind-the-scenes influence whenever the game was in difficulties. From 1977 to 1989 Lord Home was Governor of I Zingari. The general opinion is that, even if he had devoted himself to the game, he would not have been a regular county player, but then no one expected him to rise so high in politics either. H.S. Altham, in his review of public-schools cricket in the 1923 *Wisden*, said Lord Dunglass was a better batsman on wet pitches – he had the courage of his convictions and could hook and pull the turning ball effectively. Much the same could be said for his politics: he was always at his best on a sticky wicket.

HONE, SIR BRIAN, OBE, who died in Paris on May 28, 1978, aged 70, was the noted Australian educationalist who enjoyed a brief but successful first-class cricket career between 1928 and leaving his home city, Adelaide, as its 1930 Rhodes Scholar. In that time, Sir Brian scored 860 runs at an average of 50.58, including three excellent Sheffield Shield centuries. A determined player, possessed of a good defence, he won cricket and tennis Blues at Oxford and, on joining the staff of Marlborough College as head of the English Department, he played with success for Wiltshire in the Minor Counties Competition when the opportunity presented itself, topping the side's batting averages between 1937 and 1939. Returning to Australia as Headmaster of Sydney's Cranbrook School in 1940, Sir Brian became Headmaster of Melbourne Grammar School in 1950, a post he filled with distinction until retirement in 1970. He was later to be Deputy Chancellor of Monash University in 1973–74 and Chairman of the Commonwealth Secondary Schools Libraries Committee between 1971 and 1974.

HOOD, REAR-ADMIRAL THE HON. HORACE LAMBERT ALEXANDER, RN, CB, DSO, MVO, born 1870, lost his flagship, the *Queen Mary*, in the Battle of Jutland, May 31, 1916. Was a very keen, if not very distinguished cricketer. When in command of a battleship he always endeavoured to secure good cricketers as the officers of his ward and gun-rooms. When in command of the *Hyacinth* he was captain

of the officers' team, which included C.H. Abercrombie (who perished with him), and Lieut. F.W.B. Wilson, who had played at Lord's for the Navy, and was the all-round 'star' player.

HOOPER, THE REV. ROBERT POOLE, died at Hove, September 12, 1918, in his 92nd year. Played for Cambridge University v. Harrow in 1848; and was asked to play v. Oxford, but 'had already made previous promises for matches which I could not honourably throw over'. Stroke of the first Trinity boat for two years. Norfolk County Cricket XI. Considered the finest left-hand tennis player of his generation.

HORLICK, LIEUT.-COL. SIR JAMES NOCKELLS, BT, who died on the Isle of Gigha on December 31, 1972, aged 86, was in the Eton XI in 1904, taking six wickets for 90 runs against Harrow at Lord's. Though he did not get a Blue at Oxford, he played for Gloucestershire between 1907 and 1910. He served with the Coldstream Guards during the First World War in France, the Balkans and South Russia, being four times Mentioned in Dispatches and awarded the Military Cross, the Legion of Honour and the White Eagle of Serbia.

HORNUNG, ERNEST WILLIAM, who died at St Jean-de-Luz, Basses-Pyrénées, on March 22, 1921, aged 54, was a keen cricketer, but was not in the XI whilst at Uppingham. He married a sister of Sir A. Conan Doyle.

HOWELL, 2ND LIEUT. JOHN (KING'S ROYAL RIFLE CORPS), was killed in Flanders on September 25, 1915. Among all the young cricketers who have fallen in the War not one of brighter promise than John Howell can be named. Judging from his wonderful record at Repton it is not too much to say that he was potentially an England batsman. But for the War he would have been at Oxford last year and would no doubt have been seen in the Surrey XI at The Oval. Born on July 5, 1895, he was only 20 when he lost his life. He was in the Repton team for four seasons – 1911 to 1914 – being captain in 1914. From the first he showed great promise as a batsman, his style having obviously been modelled on that of Tom Hayward. He did well in 1911 and 1912, and in the next two years he was probably the best school bat in England. In 1913 he scored 737 runs for Repton, with an average of 56, and in 1914, 686 runs with an average of 52. He took some little time to find his form in school cricket in 1914, but he scored 202 not out against the Old Reptonians and 202 against Uppingham. In a trial match at The Oval at the beginning of the season he played an innings of 109. In 1913 he scored 108 and 114 against the Old Reptonians, and 144 for Young Surrey Amateurs against Young Essex Amateurs. Towards the close of the season in 1913 he journeyed up to Walsall with Surrey's Second XI for the express purpose of playing against Barnes's bowling and had the satisfaction of scoring 45.

HUNTER, GEORGE JAMES, of Staines, who died on July 14, 1943, aged 84, left his *Wisden Almanacks* from 1880 to 1942 to his Stock Exchange friend Mr John Keeble Guy. Mr Hunter was a keen club cricketer and an enthusiastic follower of the game. Mr Guy ran the Reigate Priory club for ten years and played also for Essex Second XI.

HYLAND, FREDERICK J., who died in February, 1964, aged 70, played as a professional in one match for Hampshire in 1924. Cricket in this game, at Northampton, was limited by rain to two overs from which Northamptonshire scored one run without loss. Hyland later earned a reputation as a nurseryman in Cheshire.

HYLTON, LESLIE G., died in Jamaica on May 17, 1955, aged 50. He played in six Test matches for West Indies. A fast bowler for

Jamaica, he helped in the winning of the rubber against R.E.S. Wyatt's team in the West Indies in 1934–35 when, in four Tests, he dismissed 13 batsmen at an average cost of 19.30. In 1939, he visited England under the captaincy of R.S. Grant, being chosen for two of the Test matches, but met with moderate success.

HYNDMAN, HENRY MAYERS, died at his home in Hampstead on the morning of November 22, 1921. Mr Hyndman, so well known as a Socialist leader, had some claim to be remembered for his powers in the cricket field. While up at Cambridge he only just missed getting his Blue in 1864. In his first book of recollections he admitted that in later life many things of greater moment caused him far less disappointment. He was very pleased one night at his club to hear the opinion expressed that he ought to have been chosen. Still, Cambridge were rich in run-getters in 1864, and Mr Hyndman's best score in the three trial matches in which he took part was 35 against the Free Foresters. He was one of the Trustees of Cambridge who played against Surrey at The Oval, a drawn game producing 1,104 runs – a huge aggregate in those days. Mr Hyndman kept up his cricket for several years, playing a good deal for Sussex and the Gentlemen of Sussex. He was clearly at his best in 1864. In August that year he scored at Brighton 58 against Hampshire and 62 against Middlesex, the latter innings enabling Sussex to gain a hard-won victory by three wickets. In his first book of recollections Mr Hyndman had a good deal to say about cricket, paying a high tribute to Buttress, the famous slow bowler. Born on March 7, 1842, he was in his 80th year at the time of his death.

I

ISAAC, CAPT. JOHN EDMUND VALENTINE, DSO (2ND BATT. RIFLE BRIGADE), was born in February, 1880, and killed in action in France on May 9, 1915, having previously been Mentioned in Dispatches, and wounded on October 24. He was not in the XI whilst at Harrow, but played occasionally for Worcestershire in 1907 and 1908, and had been a member of the M.C.C. since 1903. His name will occasionally be found in Free Foresters matches. During the South African campaign he was severely wounded at Nooitgedacht in December, 1900. He was a well-known gentleman jockey, and in 1911 rode the winner of the Cairo Grand National.

J

JEEVES, PERCY (ROYAL WARWICKSHIRE REGIMENT), was killed on July 22, 1916, England losing a cricketer of whom very high hopes had been entertained. Jeeves was born at Earlsheaton, in Yorkshire, on March 5, 1888. He played his first serious cricket for the Goole C.C., and became a professional at Hawes. He took part in Yorkshire trial matches in 1910, but presumably failed to attract much attention. Soon afterwards he went to live in Warwickshire, playing for that county, when not fully qualified, against the Australians and South Africans in 1912. No special success rewarded him in those matches, but in 1913 he did brilliant work for Warwickshire, both as bowler and batsman, and firmly established his position. He took 106 wickets in first-class matches that season at a cost of 20.88 each, and scored 765 runs with an average of 20.13.

In 1914 he held his own as a bowler, taking 90 wickets in first-class matches, but in batting he was less successful than before. He was chosen for Players against Gentlemen at The Oval, and by his fine bowling helped the Players to win the match, sending down in the Gentlemen's second innings 15 overs for 44 runs and four wickets. Mr P.F. Warner was greatly impressed and predicted that Jeeves would be an England bowler in the near future. Within a month War had been declared. Jeeves was a right-handed bowler on the quick side of medium pace, and with an easy action came off the ground with plenty of spin. He was very popular among his brother players.

JELLICOE, ADMIRAL OF THE FLEET, EARL, OM, GCB, GCVO, who died on November 20, 1935, aged 75, was a member of M.C.C. and I. Zingari. He captained a team of Admirals on the cricket field against the Nautical College at Pangbourne in 1930. Born on December 5, 1859, he was a very good fieldsman at cover. In 1919 Admiral Jellicoe was elected at the Annual General Meeting an Honorary Member of the M.C.C.

JENNER-FUST, HERBERT, the oldest of cricketers, passed away on July 30, 1904. The veteran, who played his first match at Lord's for Eton against Harrow in 1822, and was president of M.C.C. in 1833, was born on February 23, 1806, and was thus in his 99th year. He was the last survivor of the first Oxford and Cambridge match in 1827, and, owing to the calls of his profession, retired from first-class cricket the year before Queen Victoria came to the throne. Still, though nothing was seen of him in great matches after 1836, he played cricket in a more modest way for a long time, and made his last appearance in the field very late in life. It is interesting to recall the fact that when, in 1877, a dinner was given to celebrate the Jubilee of the University Match he was one of the chief speakers, and referred to the changes that had come over the game in 50 years.

In his cricket days he was known simply as Herbert Jenner, the additional name of Fust being taken after he had in a practical sense done with the game. Up to a short time before his death he was in such excellent health and had preserved his faculties so well – nothing but deafness troubling him – that there seemed every reason to think he would live to complete his hundred years. A letter from him towards the end of 1901 revealed no sign of extreme old age, the hand-writing being quite firm and clear. It is a curious fact that though he retained a keen interest in cricket he never took the trouble to see W.G. Grace play.

JUDGE, PETER FRANCIS, who died on March 4, 1992, aged 75, was a skilful fastish medium right-arm bowler who made a remarkable entry into first-class cricket as a 17-year-old in August 1933, only weeks after he had left St Paul's School. Middlesex gave him a game against Surrey at The Oval; he took five for 77 in 37 overs and four for 62, one of the best first-class debuts a bowler has ever had. In the next game, against Derbyshire at Lord's, he rapidly dismissed the first three batsmen and finished with an analysis of 20-10-27-5. Everything after that was an anticlimax. He only played a handful of matches the following year and then disappeared from the first-class game until 1939 when he became a professional for Glamorgan, taking 69 wickets, including eight for 75 against Yorkshire at Bradford. In the war, he was in the RAF and played some first-class cricket in India. In 1946, Judge had the bizarre experience of being dismissed for nought twice inside a minute. In the game against the Indians at Cardiff, he was bowled by C.T. Sarwate at the end of the first innings, at which point Glamorgan followed on. But with little time left, the captain Johnnie Clay decided to give the crowd some entertainment, so he waived the ten minutes between innings, and reversed his batting order. The batsmen then at the crease stayed out there and Sarwate bowled Judge again, first ball.

KEEBLE, FRANK HENRY GAMBLE, who died in New York City on August 19, 1925, was a fair batsman who played with the Staten Island C.C. He was a well-known art critic, and was born in London on June 10, 1867.

KERR, SIMON, who was found stabbed to death in a flat in Bristol on March 17, 1974, performed the extraordinary feat of scoring, when 19, five not out centuries in six innings for St George's College, Salisbury, in 1972. (See *Wisden* 1973, page 134.) The following year he paid his own fare from Rhodesia, joined the Gloucestershire ground staff and lived in the pavilion on the Bristol ground. He played for the Second XI. He was recommended to the county by M.J. Procter, the South African Test match all-rounder.

KHAN, BARKATULLAH, who died of cancer in October 1996, aged 29, was a fast-medium bowler who took 263 first-class wickets for Karachi and National Bank. As a youngster, he took 66 wickets for National Bank when they won the Quaid-e-Azam Trophy in 1986–87. He toured Zimbabwe that year with the Pakistan B team. Barkatullah played on until 1993–94 despite a serious leg injury – reportedly caused when he hit it on the corner of his bed. Doctors eventually recommended amputation, an option he rejected.

KILDEY, EDWARD KEITH, who died on February 12, 2005, aged 85, was a tall fast bowler who took just one first-class wicket: Len Hutton. His only match was for Tasmania against M.C.C. in 1946–47, and he had Hutton caught at square leg off a mistimed hook. Kildey was in the Royal Australian Air Force for nearly 30 years and, when the 1956 Olympics were held in Melbourne, was one of a group of servicemen drafted into the clay-pigeon shooting as non-scoring competitors, because of a shortage of entrants. It was later whispered to him that, had he been eligible, he would have won the bronze medal.

KUBUNAVANUA, PETERO, who died on November 20, 1997, became a first-class cricketer retrospectively when the Fijian tour of New Zealand in 1947–48 was given first-class status more than 30 years later. He was a dashing left-handed bat and spectacular outfielder whose saves and spear-like throwing, barefoot and with his *sulu* (knee-length skirt) flying, delighted the crowds. His fielding action was depicted on a postage stamp to mark the centenary of cricket in Fiji. Kubunavanua had a fine solo voice and performed in concert halls on the tour; he made an impressive sight as well, with a ferocious countenance under a bush of hair. After fighting the Japanese in the Solomon Islands, he served in Malaya. Fielding at square leg in a state match there, he was irritated by a swallow flying round him, stuck out his hand, and put the bird in his *sulu* pocket.

KUMAR, SIVA SHANTHI, was shot dead while playing golf at the Royal Colombo club on December 7, 1996, aged 53. Two gunmen climbed a wall and fired six shots at him on the 12th green. Shanthi Kumar was captain of the Tamil Union team in the early 1970s.

LACY, GEORGE, a great lover of cricket, and at one time a well-known critic, died on November 3, 1904, at Grafton House, East Sandgate, Kent. He was born in Surrey in 1844, and had followed the game closely in many parts of the world. His articles on 'Present-Day Cricket', which appeared in *Cricket* in 1897, attracted much attention. He was one of the very few men who could claim to have walked across Africa from East to West before the first Boer War. He was best known in the literary world as the author of *Liberty and Law*.

LANE, JOHN HENRY HERVEY VINCENT, of King's Bromley Manor, Lichfield, died on February 22, 1917, aged 49. A keen cricketer and a member of M.C.C. since 1900. A direct descendent of Mr Thomas Lane, the country gentleman who assisted Charles II to escape after the Battle of Worcester.

LEAR, THE VENERABLE FRANCIS (LATE ARCHDEACON OF SARUM), who died at Salisbury on February 19, 1914, was born at Dounton, Wilts, on August 23, 1823, and was thus one of the oldest of cricketers. At Winchester, where he was contemporary with V.C. Smith and Fred Gale, he was in the XI in 1841, scoring 0 and 1 v. Harrow, and 1 and 11 v. Eton. In 1843 and 1844 he played for Oxford against Cambridge, scoring 1 and 6 in the former year and 6 in the latter. He lived practically all his life in the Salisbury diocese and served under six Bishops.

LE COUTEUR, PHILIP RIDGEWAY, who died in Australia on June 30, 1958, aged 73, did fine work as an all-rounder for Oxford University, where he was a Rhodes Scholar, in the early part of the century. From Melbourne University he went to Oxford in 1908 and appeared in the XI in the three following seasons. He fared moderately in his first match against Cambridge, but in 1910 enjoyed pronounced success. He played an innings of 160 and, in taking six wickets for 20 and five for 46, bore a leading part in the dismissal of the Light Blues for 76 and 113 and their defeat in an innings with 126 runs to spare. Next season he took eight wickets for 99 in the second innings and helped Oxford to victory by 74 runs. In 1910 and 1911 he made six appearances for Gentlemen against Players. A batsman who excelled in back-play and on-side strokes, he also bowled leg-breaks skilfully with deceptive variation of pace. After leaving Oxford, he studied psychology for two years at the University of Bonn, returning in 1913 to Australia, where he became lecturer in philosophy at the University of Western Australia. He made two or three appearances for Victoria without achieving distinction.

LEWIS, GERALD, who was killed in a road accident on January 26, 2000, aged 62, was a fanatical walker. His obsession bewildered and entranced spectators at Queen's Park Oval, Port of Spain. At a ferocious pace, he would march around the boundary before play, afterwards and during the intervals, proudly carrying the Trinidad & Tobago flag ahead of him. He repeated this at other major sporting events and constituted a minor national institution. Lewis was killed on his way home from a cricket match at Pointe-à-Pierre when a taxi hit his bicycle.

LITHGOW, LIEUT.-COL. WILLIAM SAMUEL PLENDERLEATH, who died on August 8, 1997, aged 77, played for Oxford in 1939 but did not gain a Blue. Later, asked what he had read, he said cricket and rugger. He became a highly successful *chef d'équipe* and chairman of selectors of the British Olympic equestrian team.

LITTLE, ALFRED ALEXANDER, died in Media, Pennsylvania on August 14, 2002, aged 77. He had been curator of the C.C. Morris Cricket Library at Haverford College, which houses a renowned collection of American memorabilia. Little, a mechanical engineer, worked on developing a nose cone for intercontinental ballistic missiles in the 1950s and later joined the Corona project, which devised ways of taking military surveillance photos from space.

LLOYD, NEIL, who died at Wakefield, of an unidentified virus, on September 17, 1982, aged 17, was a left-handed batsman of great promise. He had played for three years for Yorkshire Second XI and barely a fortnight before his death had gone in first for Young England against Young West Indies in the third of last season's 'Test' matches. He was awarded his Yorkshire Second XI cap posthumously.

LONGBOURNE, CAPT. HUGH RICHARD, DSO (Queen's Royal West Surrey Regiment), killed May, 1916. Repton XI, 1901–03. Received the Russian Order of St Stanislaus with Swords.

DE LUGO, ANTHONY BENITEZ, MARQUIS DE SANTA LUSANA, a well-known member of the Surrey County C.C., died at Pau on March 16, 1907, aged about 50. He was author of three booklets published in Madrid for private circulation – *Surrey at the Wicket, 1844–1887, The Surrey Companion: A Complete Record of W.W. Read's Performances, 1873–1894*, and *A Summary of Surrey Cricket, 1844–1899*.

LYON, BEVERLEY HAMILTON, who died on June 22, 1970, aged 68, was one of the most astute captains of his era. Of Surrey birth, he was in the Rugby XI in 1917 and 1918, heading the batting averages in the second year, when his highest innings was 98 not out and he represented Lord's Schools against The Rest. Going up to Oxford in 1920, he gained a Blue in 1922 but failed to score in either innings in the University match, which Cambridge won by an innings and 100 runs. On the big occasion the following season, he gained some recompense, for although he scored no more than 14, an immensely powerful Oxford team this time triumphed in two days with an innings and 227 runs to spare.

In 1921, Lyon began his association with Gloucestershire. He became captain in 1929, a position which he filled for four seasons, and under his inspiring influence the county enjoyed greater success than for many years. T.W. Goddard, whose services as a fast bowler had been dispensed with by Gloucestershire, had joined the ground-staff at Lord's and become an off-break exponent. Lyon recalled him to the county and between them Goddard and the left-arm C.W.L. Parker developed into the most effective spin-bowling combination in the Championship.

Lyon also played his part as a hard-hitting batsman. He hit 1,397 runs, including three centuries, in 1929 for an average of over 33 and next season obtained 1,355 runs, averaging 41.00. In 1930 he hit two of his total of 16 centuries – 115 and 101 not out – in the match with Essex at Bristol, and he enjoyed the distinction of helping his county to a tie with W.M. Woodfull's Australian team.

Lyon, known as an apostle of brighter cricket, was revolutionary in his cricket outlook. He was the originator in 1931 of the scheme by which a declaration by each side with only four byes scored in the first innings enabled maximum points to be available to the winning county after the loss of the opening two days of a Championship match through rain. This caused the Advisory County Cricket Committee to revise the regulations. He was the first to suggest first-class county games on Sundays, an idea which it took 36 years for the authorities to adopt. He also advanced the scheme for a knock-out competition, which came into being over 30 years afterwards. There was no funeral for Beverley Lyon, for he bequeathed his body to the Royal College of Surgeons.

M

MACKINNON OF MACKINNON, THE (35TH CHIEF OF THE
MACKINNON CLAN), the title to which Mr Francis Alexander
Mackinnon succeeded on the death of his father in 1903, passed
away at his home, Drumduan, in Forres, Morayshire, on February
27, 1947. He would have been 99 years old on April 9. As it was he
reached a greater age than attained by any other first-class cricketer,
surpassing that of Herbert Jenner-Fust, Cambridge captain in the
first match with Oxford in 1827, who died in 1904 when his exact
age was 98 years five months and seven days. Mackinnon was within
40 days of 99 years at his passing.

Born at Acryse Park, in Kent, he went to Harrow without getting into the XI, but at Cambridge he played in the historic match
of 1870 when Cobden did the hat-trick by dismissing the last three
Oxford batsmen and gaining for the Light Blues a dramatic victory
by two runs. He played 10 years for Kent, and in 1884, going in
first, he helped, with scores of 28 and 29, in the only victory gained
by a county over the Australians. Of the winning side, Mr Stanley
Christopherson, President of M.C.C. during the war years, who
finished the match by taking three wickets for 12 runs, Mr M.C.
Kemp, wicket-keeper, and Alec Hearne, seven wickets for 60, are
three survivors of that XI.

In the winter of 1878 he went with Lord Harris to Australia. A
strong batting side included only two professionals, George Ulyett
and Tom Emmett, the Yorkshiremen. Mackinnon was a victim of
F.R. Spofforth in a hat-trick in the only match with the full strength
of Australia, who won by 10 wickets.

Born on April 9, 1848, three months before W.G. Grace, he married in 1888 the eldest daughter of Admiral, first Baron Hood, the

Hon. Emily Hood, who died in 1934. There survive a son and a daughter, who accompanied her father on his cricket visits to the South.

The oldest Harrovian, University Blue and Test cricketer, he was also the senior member of M.C.C., to which he was elected in 1870. Until the last he retained a keen interest in the game he loved so well by following the reports of the matches played by the England team in Australia. Although he gave up county cricket 62 years ago, he maintained to a remarkable extent a close touch with the game, as his memory and good physique gave evidence. Using two sticks, he walked firmly, and enjoyed meeting old friends on Kent grounds as well as at Lord's. During the Tunbridge Wells Cricket Week in 1946 he watched the cricket from the Band of Brothers' tent or from the pavilion. One afternoon, accompanied by his daughter and the Marchioness of Abergavenny, he visited Rose Hill School and examined the old desk where he used to sit as a pupil 89 years before. He gave a talk to the whole school, besides inspecting the Sea Scout Troop. Several opportunities occurred for me to speak to the Mackinnon, and he related some of his experiences in the happiest way. He liked Canterbury better even than Lord's, his second love. An amusing tale was how, at The Oval when playing for Kent, Lord Harris put him to field at a particular spot – "'Mac, by that worm cast." After some hits just out of reach, my captain said: "You have left your cast." "No, George, I haven't. That's another worm's cast."' Referring to 'Cobden's Match', he said with a smile, 'I really won the match, for I scored two' (the margin of victory). That was his second innings, after a useful 17 not out at a time when runs were never more difficult to get than at Lord's on the big occasion.

Among those who chatted with him in the Lord Harris Memorial garden, where he enjoyed a picnic lunch with his daughter during the University match, was the Rev. T.R. Hine Haycock, an Oxford Blue in 1883, who played for Kent when Mackinnon was finishing his active cricket career and is now 85 years old.

Mackinnon wore an I Zingari tie, and on his watch-chain showed with pride a gold medallion bearing the insignia of crossed bats presented to all the team captained by Lord Harris in Australia. His wonderfully clear conversation and strong handshake revealed his hearty enjoyment in meeting any cricket acquaintance. Among the last active signs of his fondness for the game was the presentation to Canterbury of a picture of the Kent and Sussex match at Hove 100 years ago, in which the players, among them Alfred Mynn, 'the Lion of Kent', and Fuller Pilch, are wearing tall hats.

When 98 years of age, in reply to a question by telephone from London as to his health, he said: 'I am going into hospital tomorrow – but only for the annual meeting at which I shall preside. I am very well in health – very well indeed. I still do a lot of work in the garden: weeds don't like me at all.'

MACLAGAN, MYRTLE ETHEL, MBE, who died at Farnham on March 11, 1993, aged 81, was one of the best-known women cricketers of her day. She was in the cricket team at the Royal School, Bath, for six years and, having been coached by Tich Freeman, took five wickets in five balls with her off-breaks against Cheltenham Ladies College. She became a national personality after being chosen for the pioneering tour of Australia in 1934–35. In the first Test at Brisbane she made 72 and took seven for ten; in the second game at Sydney she made 119, the first hundred in a women's Test. England's men had just lost the Ashes but soon Maclagan's opening partnership with Betty Snowball was being compared to Hobbs and Sutcliffe, and the *Morning Post* published the following quatrain:

What matter that we lost, mere nervy men
Since England's women now play England's game,
Wherefore Immortal *Wisden*, take your pen
And write MACLAGAN on the scroll of fame.

MacLagan made another century against Australia in 1937, toured again in 1948–49 and captained England in two Tests at home in 1951. She was an officer in the ATS during the war and rejoined the Army in 1951, becoming Inspector, PT for the WRAC. Her last major match was against the Australian touring team for the Combined Services in 1963, when she scored 81 not out. She was 52. In 1966 she was appointed MBE. At various times in her life she won prizes for squash, tennis, badminton and knitting. It was reported that so many people turned up for her 80th birthday she had to make a speech from the top of a step-ladder and got attention by a blast on her whistle.

MAKANT, CAPT. ROBERT KEITH, who was born on June 28, 1895, was murdered whilst on duty in Kurdistan on June 18, 1922. He was in the Harrow XI in 1913 and 1914, and in his two matches with Eton scored four and 46, four and 14 obtained five wickets, but on each occasion was on the losing side. He bowled slow from a great height, and in 1913 headed the averages with a record of 23 wickets for 16.06 runs each. During the First World War he was wounded, and he gained the MC and Bar whilst serving with the Royal North Lancashire Regiment.

MALIK, SARDAR HARDIT SINGH, CIF, OBE, died at Delhi in October, 1985, aged 90. Educated in England from the age of eight, he headed the batting averages at Eastbourne College and, going up to Balliol, attracted attention in the Freshmen's match in 1913 and in the Seniors' match in 1914 but did not have a game for the University. However, playing five matches for Sussex in August, 1914, he scored 71 against Leicestershire and 49 against Middlesex and showed himself fully up to first-class form. He was in fact playing for Sussex in the Canterbury Week when war was declared on August 4, and at the time of his death he was the last survivor of the Week before 1919. After gallant service in the Royal Flying Corps during the war, in which he was shot down and wounded, he returned to Oxford for a year in 1920, played a second time in the Varsity golf match and had a trial in the cricket side without success. For Sussex, however in the Horsham Week he played a brilliant innings of 106 against Leicestershire. He and Albert Reif put on 175 for the seventh wicket at a tremendous pace.

He played no county cricket after 1921, but his turbaned figure was for many years a familiar sight on English golf courses when the demands of a distinguished career in the Indian diplomatic service, where he was his country's first High Commissioner to Canada and later their Ambassador in Paris, allowed. A man of great charm, he was widely loved.

MAGUIRE, AIR MARSHAL SIR HAROLD JOHN, KCB, DSO, OBE, at one time Director-General of Intelligence at the Ministry of Defence, died on February 1, 2001, aged 88. In 1959, after flying a Spitfire over Whitehall as part of the Battle of Britain commemorations, he was forced to come down at Bromley. Showing commendable discernment, he avoided *The Times*' sports ground and elected to crash-land instead on the OXO cricket pitch, splintering the stumps. Fortunately the players were having tea in the pavilion, where the intrepid pilot joined them for a reviving cuppa.

MANNING, CARDINAL, died on January 14, 1892, aged 83. It may seem a little strange to include Cardinal Manning's name in a cricket obituary, but inasmuch as he played for Harrow against Winchester at Lord's in 1825, in the first match that ever took place between the two schools, his claim cannot be disputed.

MASTERMAN, SIR JOHN CECIL, sometime Provost of Worcester and Vice-Chancellor of Oxford University, died in an Oxford nursing home on June 6, 1977, aged 86. A man of distinction in many walks of life, he was a remarkable games player, who had played hockey and lawn tennis for England, won the high jump in the University sports and reached a high standard at cricket, golf and squash. 'Cricket', he wrote, 'was my first and most enduring passion', and, though never near a Blue at Oxford, he became a formidable club player, good enough to be elected a Harlequin many years after he went down and to play for both Harlequins and Free Foresters against the University, to do valuable work for Oxfordshire from 1922 to 1925 and to be a member of the M.C.C. side to Canada in 1937. He was a sound left-handed bat and, being a good fighter, one whom one was always glad to have on one's side when things were not going well, and a right-hand medium-pace bowler with a rather low and clumsy action, but very steady and reliable. For many years he was on the committee of both I Zingari and Free Foresters. He enjoyed writing on the game and did so delightfully, but a busy life left him little time for this. His novel, *Fate Cannot Harm Me*, contains one of the best descriptions extant of a country-house match and there is an interesting chapter on cricket in his autobiography, *On the Chariot Wheel*. Besides these there is a sketch of W.E.W. Collins in *Bits and Pieces* and a fascinating article contributed to *Blackwood* in June 1974 on that remarkable character, Captain E.G. Wynyard.

MAUDE, JOHN, died on November 17, 1934, aged 84, having been born on March 17, 1850. Going to Eton when ten as a colleger, he was there for nine years under three headmasters – Goodford, Balston and Hornby. His tutor was the Rev. J.E. Yonge. In his time he had three future Bishops as fags – Welldon (Calcutta), Ryle (Liverpool) and Harmer (Rochester).

He played in the Eton XI at Lord's as a medium left-hand bowler in 1868 and 1869. In the former year, when Harrow won, he took three wickets for 20 runs. Lord Harris, who was also a member of the team, wrote in his recollections of the match, 'Our best bowler was John Maude, who probably did not bowl nearly enough.' In 1869 Maude, by taking seven wickets for 36 in the second innings, contributed largely to Eton's victory by an innings and 19 runs. Of that famous match Mr H.S. Salt, in his *Memories of Bygone Eton*, wrote: 'C.J. Ottaway made a century. Thanks mainly to his patient and skilful batting and to some fine left-hand bowling by John Maude, the match ended in a single-innings victory for Eton. Old Stephen Hawtrey is said to have stopped Maude in the street and asked to be allowed to shake "that noble hand" which by a wonderful "caught and bowled" had disposed of Harrow's most formidable batsman. We all believed the story. It seemed exactly what Stephen Hawtrey would have done. But 57 years later I was told by Maude that he had no recollection of the incident. It *ought* to have happened, anyhow.'

Maude also played in the Mixed Wall and Field XIs in 1868, and won the school fives in 1869. He went up to Oxford, and got his cricket Blue in 1873. At Lord's he took six Cambridge wickets for 39 runs in the second innings. On the first day he caught F.E.R. Fryer, the Light Blue captain, in sensational fashion. He was a member of the Harlequins, and played for the Gentlemen of Warwickshire in 1874.

MAULE, THE REV. DR WARD, of the Cambridge XI of 1853, died at Boulogne-sur-Mer on September 23, 1913. He was born September 1, 1833, was educated at Tonbridge, and appeared occasionally for the Gentlemen of Kent. At Tunbridge Wells in 1854, whilst bowling at practice to Fuller Pilch before the match between Kent and 18 of Tunbridge Wells, he took the single stump three times in successive balls. 'Oh! sir,' said Pilch, 'I should not have believed it possible.' In his one match against Oxford he scored seven and 14 not out, and took three wickets. 'He *wards* his own wicket, while he *mauls* those of others,' once said a well-known cricketer.

McCUBBIN, MAJOR GEORGE REYNOLDS, who died at Johannesburg on May 9, 1944, aged 46, took part in two first-class matches, both for Transvaal against Rhodesia in March 1923. In the second of these, at Bulawayo, batting No. 10, he scored 97, adding 221 for the ninth wicket with N.V. Lindsay (160 not out), a South African record for that wicket which still stands. A pilot in the R.F.C. in the last war, he was awarded the D.S.O., and won fame in June 1916 when he shot down the famous German ace, Max Immelmann. He served with the South African Air Force in North Africa in the present war, but had to retire owing to ill-health.

MCRAE, TEMP. SURGEON LIEUT. F.M., RNVR, was killed when H.M.S. *Mahratta*, a destroyer, was lost in February, 1944. Playing first for Somerset in 1936, he steadily improved in batting, although not finding time for regular participation in first-class cricket, and in 1939 he averaged 30.40, his best innings being 107 against Hampshire at Taunton – his only century for the county. He fielded very smartly. At St Mary's Hospital he made a name as a dashing three-quarter and appeared in a Rugby international trial. His death at the age of 28 was a great loss to Somerset, as expressed by Brigadier Lancaster, Hon. Secretary to the county.

MENZIES, SIR ROBERT GORDON, the famous Australian statesman, who died at his home in Melbourne on May 15, 1978, aged 83, was a very great lover of cricket indeed and had much to say in his auto-biography, *Afternoon Light*, on how much it had meant to him. A close friend of many of the Australian players, between 1965, when he was appointed Lord Warden of the Cinque Ports, and the break-down of his health in 1971, he spent much of each summer in England and was constantly to be found watching, specially on Kent grounds. He was President of the Kent County Cricket Club in 1968 and was a member of I Zingari and of the Band of Brothers.

MILLAR, CHARLES CHRISTIAN HOYER, founder and for 55 years pres-ident of Rosslyn Park Rugby Football Club, who died on

November 22, 1942, aged 81, deserved mention in *Wisden* for a very special and unique reason. He undertook on his own initiative to weed Lord's turf, and Sir Francis Lacey, secretary of M.C.C., signed a deed of appointment making him Honorary Weedkiller to G.H.Q. Cricket. From 1919 to 1931 he kept up his task, being particularly busy on summer evenings after stumps were drawn, and his zeal often received comment from pressmen walking to the exit when their duties were done. Mr Millar, according to his own reckoning, accounted for 624,000 victims, having spent 956 hours in his war against plantains and other unwanted vegetation.

MILLER-HALLETT, ALEXANDER, for ten successive years until 1946 President of Sussex, died at Brighton on February 14, 1953, aged 97. His cricketing connections with Sussex went back as far as 1866, and in the years before the second Great War he did much to increase the membership of the county club. Known as The Grand Old Man of Sussex Cricket, he was also a celebrated breeder of Jersey cattle. While he was watching cricket nothing else mattered. Once during a war-time match at Hove a German aircraft dropped a bomb on the ground. Without moving from his seat, Miller-Hallett remarked to his neighbour:'Fancy disturbing our game like that!'

MILLIGAN, LIEUT. FRANK W., (YORKSHIRE). Born at Aldershot, March 19, 1870, died whilst with Colonel Plummer's force (endeavouring to relieve Mafeking), March 31, 1900. An excellent all-round player, a splendid field, fast bowler, and hard hitter. Represented the Gentlemen v. the Players in 1897 and 1898. He made a successful first appearance for the Gentlemen – at The Oval in 1897 – scoring 47 and 47, and obtaining two wickets for three runs in the second innings of the Players. In the Scarborough match in 1898, he took in the second innings seven wickets for 61 runs.

MONCKTON, WALTER TURNER, FIRST VISCOUNT OF BRENCHLEY, who died on January 9, 1965, aged 73, kept wicket for Harrow against Eton in 'Fowler's match'. From 1919 to 1946 he kept wicket for the Bar, became President of M.C.C. in 1956 and was President of Surrey from 1950 to 1952 and from 1959 until his death. He gained great distinctions as a barrister and was in turn Attorney-General – a post he held at the time of the abdication of King Edward VIII in 1936 – Solicitor-General, Minister of Defence, Paymaster-General and Minister of Labour.

MOSS, SAM, reputed to have been at one time the fastest bowler in England, was killed on the railway line whilst walking to a match at Featherstone on August 7, 1923. He was in his 56th year. He was very successful for Bacup in the Lancashire League in 1899 and at least twice during his career he obtained all ten wickets in an innings – for 19 runs for Padiham in 1908 and for 32 runs for Barnsley v. Huddersfield. At various times he was also on the Old Trafford ground-staff and with the Batley C.C.

MOUNTGARRET, RT. HON. THE 17TH VISCOUNT, who died on February 7, 2004, was regarded as a comically eccentric aristocrat until events thrust him into the centre of Yorkshire's turbulent cricket politics of the 1980s. In 1984, Mountgarret – owner of a huge swathe of countryside near Harrogate – was nominated out of the blue as Yorkshire president in the midst of the club's civil war between supporters and opponents of Geoff Boycott. His arrival was farcical: the chairman, Reg Kirk, introduced him as 'Viscount Mountbatten'. But Mountgarret, himself just an enthusiastic but indifferent cricketer for the smarter touring clubs, was so far above the Yorkshire battle that he proved the ideal choice. He said he intended to 'bang heads together', and he succeeded in doing so: during his six years as president, the situation became far calmer. He was helped by being rather deaf, which meant he never had to listen to the overheated nonsense talked on both sides of the dispute. Earlier, he had been best known for a bizarre incident when he took pot-shots at a hot-air balloon that flew over his grouse moor; he was found guilty of recklessly endangering an aircraft, and fined £1,000.

NASON, CAPT. JOHN WILLIAM WASHINGTON (ROYAL FLYING CORPS), born at Corse Grange, Gloucestershire, on August 4, 1889, was killed in December, 1916. He was educated at University School, Hastings, and Cambridge, where he obtained his Blue in 1909. As a lad he was regarded as a player of unusual promise, but, although he made some useful scores both for the University and Sussex, it cannot be said that he did as well as was expected. His first appearance for Sussex, against Warwickshire at Hastings in 1906, was marked by a curious incident, for he was allowed to replace Dwyer after that player had bowled five overs, and in his second innings carried out his bat for 53. When playing for University School v. Hastings Post Office in 1908, he opened the innings and when he was bowled after batting for half an hour the score-sheet read: J.W.W. Nason b Cox, 97; L. Inskipp not out, 1; bye, 1; total (1 wkt.) 99. He obtained all the first 64 runs and hit three sixes and 14 fours.

NEWELL, ANDREW L., the well-known Australian cricketer, left home in 1907 and has not been seen or heard of in more than a year. He had been in indifferent health for some time and had been advised to take a month's holiday. It is probable that he lost his life over the sea cliffs in the vicinity of Ben Buckler, near Bondi. He was born on November 13, 1870, and was a very useful all-round player identified with the Glebe Electorate C.C. of Sydney.*

* Newell's disappearance turned out to have been deliberate; he actually died in 1915.

OATES, CAPT. LAWRENCE EDWARD GRACE, who died on March 17, 1912, his 32nd birthday, whilst returning from the South Pole with Capt. Scott's ill-fated party, played cricket for his House as a lower boy at Eton.

ODD, MONTAGU, who died at Sutton, Surrey, on June 11, 1951, aged 82, used to make cricket bats by hand for Dr W.G. Grace at a guinea apiece. He was at work in his little shop a few days before his death.

O'GORMAN, JOE G., who died at Weybridge on August 26, 1974, aged 84, was famous as the other half of a comedy act with brother Dave, but he always delighted in his cricket adventures with Surrey, which included batting with Jack Hobbs. This gave him as much pleasure as seeing his name in lights on Broadway. An all-rounder, he might well have made his mark in the game had he chosen so. He played in three Championship matches for the county in 1927, sharing with Andy Sandham a partnership of 119 in 65 minutes, against Essex. O'Gorman hit 42 of those runs, with Sandham scoring altogether 230. A slow bowler, he took a wicket with his first ball in county cricket against Glamorgan at The Oval when he dismissed W.E. Bates, the opening batsman. For many years he and his brother played club cricket for Richmond for which club he took over 1,500 wickets.

ORNSBY, JOHN ARTHUR, died at Durham on March 28, 1915, aged 64. He was in the Doncaster Grammar School XI in 1867 and two following years, being captain in 1869, when he headed the batting averages. He was also a very good long-stop. In 1870 he won the long jump for Oxford in the University Sports, covering 20ft, ¾ins, and rowed twice in the Boat Race – in 1872 and 1873, the latter being the first year in which sliding seats were used.

ORR, HERBERT RICHARD, perhaps the most prominent personality connected with Bedfordshire cricket, passed away on May 22, 1940, at the age of 75. Getting into the Bedford School XI when 15, Herbert Orr finished five years in the side as captain in 1884, and actually played his first game for the county in 1882. From that time his interest in the Bedfordshire club remained undiminished.

His devotion to the game found lasting proof in his will, by which he left 'the cricket picture, Sussex v. Kent, to his friend, Dr Alfred F. Morcom, of Belgrave Square, S.W., in memory of many pleasant days spent together in the cricket field, £100 to the Bedfordshire County C.C., and £50 to the Bedford Town C.C., in memory of my dear friend Reginald William Rice, with which clubs we have enjoyed so many pleasant games together'. Also in his gift was a fielding trophy to Bedford School, for award in the First XI. Appropriately enough, this was won two years ago by the son of Mr Frank Crompton, the present hon. secretary of the Bedfordshire County Club. He was a member of M.C.C.

After leaving Cambridge, where he just failed to get his Blue, Herbert Orr went to Australia. His ability was recognised very soon; he played for the Melbourne club and captained the first Western Australia team in 1892. Returning to England in 1899, he resumed his associations with Bedfordshire and captained the side until 1915. With him at one period was A.F. Morcom, a fast bowler, the Cambridge Blue of 1905 to 1907. In the match against Suffolk at Luton in 1908 Morcom created a record, which still stands in English cricket, by sending a bail 70¼yd. Also in the Bedfordshire XI at that time was R.W. Rice, the former Oxford University and Gloucestershire batsman.

After the First World War Herbert Orr invariably visited Australia to see the Test matches, and on one return trip to England with the Australian team he won 'The Ashes' at deck quoits. A small silver urn containing cigarette ash was inscribed with the names of the players – W.H. Ponsford and W.A. Oldfield were of the party.

P

PARAVICINI, PERCY JOHN DE, died on October 12, 1921, having undergone a surgical operation. Mr Paravicini's numberless friends were shocked at the news of his death, no mention of his illness having appeared in any of the newspapers. Few men personally more popular have ever been seen in the cricket field. His career was in one respect peculiar. He was in proportion a far greater force in his schooldays than he ever became in first-class matches.

He was in the Eton XI for four years, getting his place in 1878 and being captain in 1880–81. In those four seasons he was on the winning side three times against Winchester, but never against Harrow. His greatest triumph was the match against Winchester in 1881, when he scored 27 and 32 and took 10 wickets – five for 25 runs and five for 46. Thanks mainly to his efforts Eton beat Winchester – a side composed of abnormally tall and powerful young cricketers – by six wickets.

Going up to Cambridge after the season of 1881 Paravicini was in the University XI for four years. He was on the winning side three times at Lord's, Cambridge winning in 1882, 1883, and 1885, but losing by seven wickets to M.C. Kemp's splendid XI in 1884. In these four matches Paravicini's best score was 37. His quick bowling, so formidable at Eton, had quite left him, and in the four matches he was only put on in three innings, meeting with no success.

Though a failure as a bowler and only a partial success as a batsman, Paravicini was one of the finest outfields ever seen in the University match – very fast, untiring, and a sure catch. In this connection I remember hearing J.A. Turner say in the pavilion, when Cambridge had won the 1885 match by seven wickets, 'Para, we

didn't get any runs, but we fielded damned well.' For Middlesex Paravicini played some good innings, but in county cricket, as for Cambridge, his value lay chiefly in his splendid fielding.

As a man Paravicini earned far more distinction at Association football than at cricket. One of the best backs of his day, he was for several seasons a mainstay of the Old Etonians, and in the season of 1882–83 he played for England against Scotland, Wales, and Ireland. He was a member of the Old Etonians' team that won the Association Cup in 1882. He was born on July 15, 1862.

PATTERSON, WILLIAM HARRY, almost a life-long figure in Kent cricket, died on May 3, 1946, aged 87. An exceptionally sound and skilful batsman, he could produce his best form without previous practice in first-class cricket. For many years, owing to the calls on his time as a solicitor, he got practically no county cricket until late in the season, but then he was as likely as anyone to make a big score. He was elected captain of Kent for the second half of the season four times. Playing with a very straight bat and watching the ball carefully, he surpassed most of his amateur contemporaries on the sticky turf so often experienced in the days before pitches underwent over-elaborate preparation.

Born at the Royal Military College, Sandhurst, on March 11, 1859, Harry Patterson, after some years at school in Ramsgate, gained a place in the Harrow XI, and, proceeding to Oxford, played a big part in a victory over Cambridge by 135 runs in 1881. The Light Blues, very strong with three Studds and A.G. Steel, were expected to gain a fourth consecutive victory, but the Oxford fast bowler, A.H. Evans, took 13 wickets for ten runs apiece. His second effort came after Patterson, going in first, played so admirably for five hours, despite having a finger broken, that he carried out his bat for 107. Besides this heroic display, Patterson gave further help. Early in the innings C.F.H. Leslie played a ball back to A.F.J. Ford, who, over six feet in height, reached up, took it with one hand, and threw the ball up. Leslie walked towards the pavilion, but Patterson, not satisfied that it was a catch, appealed to Farrands, the umpire, who decided in favour of the batsman. Leslie raised a score of eight to 70.

During 20 years, from 1880, Patterson made 6,902 runs for Kent, and in three seasons his average exceeded 40, the best being 49 in 1885. He appeared for Gentlemen against Players four times in the eighties, and took part in Kent's victory over the Australians at Canterbury in 1884, the only success by a county against the touring teams of that season and 1882. At the time of Patterson's death, F.A. MacKinnon, Stanley Christopherson, M.C. Kemp and Alec Hearne were survivors of that triumphant XI. Often serving on the M.C.C. Committee – first in 1893 – he for some years was an auditor. After being Kent President he became a Vice-President and Trustee of the county club, retaining these offices until the end.

PAYNE, CHARLES, who played for Sussex from 1857 until 1870, and for Kent from 1863 until 1870, died at Tonbridge on February 18, 1909. He was born at East Grinstead on May 12, 1832, and played for Sussex by birth and for Kent by residence. In *Scores and Biographies* (v – 326) he was described as: 'A fine, free, but very steady forward player, having a great reach, besides being a good hitter, and he has made many long scores in the best matches; also a splendid field at short-leg, in fact he was considered the 'best cut' at that post.' In a match against Hastings at Tunbridge Wells in 1863 he hit a ball from the late John Sands for which 13 were run, but when he scored 122 against XXII of Richmond in 1867 his first 26 runs were all singles. His highest score for Sussex was 137 v. M.C.C. and Ground at Brighton in 1867, and for Kent 135 not out v. Surrey at Gravesend in 1866. He played for England and for the South of England XI, but never, curiously enough, for the Players. When England met Surrey at The Oval in 1866 he was sent in first and made 86; 'W.G.', then 18 years old, scored 224 not out, he and Payne adding 135 for the fourth wicket. For several seasons Payne, who belonged to a well-known cricketing family, umpired in first-class matches and gave the greatest satisfaction.

PEARCE, PERCY (familiarly known as Peter), who from 1874 to 1898 was Ground Superintendent at Lord's, died suddenly at Hither Green, on Tuesday, August 22, 1911. He was born on September 2, 1843, at Shipley, Sussex. For some time he was gaining experience in the making and upkeep of lawns under the direction of Mr Sydney Ford, of Leonardslee, Sussex. The first cricket ground of which he had charge was the present County Ground at Brighton. On November 9, 1874, Pearce was appointed to Lord's, being the successful applicant out of over 400 candidates.

About this period the condition of Lord's must have been very bad. The *Saturday Review* in its report of the University of 1873 said: 'We must add in conclusion that very little can be said in favour of the wickets provided for this match. There has not been a single good wicket at Lord's as yet this season . . . It is almost an insult to common sense to suppose that a Club with an income of ten thousand a year cannot find the means of covering half-a-dozen acres with turf adapted to the game of cricket . . . There are other clubs in London whose committees can provide wickets for any number of great matches, on which cricketers may play without any fear of their teeth being knocked down their throats, or their arms being disabled.'

Pearce went to Lord's in the winter of 1874, and a new order of things soon came to pass. The *Field*, reporting the Gentlemen v. Players match of 1876, said: 'There is a certain amount of novelty attached to the idea of a cricket ground being "too good" for the purpose of a great match, yet such an idea is entertained by the Marylebone Club, and Pearce has orders not to improve it further . . . Better wickets than those of Monday were not needed, and to their condition the heavy scoring may in a large degree be attributed.' The *Standard* of June 27, 1876, speaking of the University game said: 'Time was when a good Wicket at Lord's was the exception, but now, happily – thanks to Pearce, the groundsman – the playing portion of the arena is in faultless condition, and a batsman can concentrate his energies on the defence of his "timber" without, as formerly, having any misgiving as to his personal safety.'

Pearce's death was due to syncope, and the funeral took place on August 26, 1911, at Ladywell Cemetery. He left a widow, three sons, and a daughter. His eldest son, a promising cricketer who had played for the Sussex Colts, and had wonderful records in India, was killed in the South African war.

PEPPER, CECIL GEORGE, who died on March 24, 1993, aged 74, was a leg-spinner often described as the best Australian player never to win a Test cap. He was, without any doubt, one of the greatest characters ever to come near the game, to whom anecdotes clung, as with Fred Trueman, some of them actually true. He played 16 matches for New South Wales before the Sheffield Shield closed down for the war, building a reputation as a big spinner of the ball, a great exponent of the flipper, and a hitter of devastating power. Next to Keith Miller he was the big attraction of the 1945 Australian Services team in England and he emulated C.I. Thornton's 1886 hit by smashing Eric Hollies over the houses at Scarborough and into Trafalgar Square. It was assumed he would soon play for Australia but a few months later at Adelaide he exchanged words with umpire Jack Scott, after Scott had turned down three appeals against Bradman. He left Australia to play League cricket for seven different clubs in Lancashire, Cheshire and Staffordshire.

He never did learn to keep quiet and it made him one of League cricket's great drawcards. A *Manchester Evening News* correspondent said he could not imagine any match involving Pepper pursuing a peaceful course. Usually there was more humour than anger, though when he went to India with the 1949–50 Commonwealth side he had to leave early because the umpiring annoyed him so much.

It was thus gloriously ironic that in 1964 he became a first-class umpire. For 16 seasons he mixed an irreverent manner with a fearless if occasionally idiosyncratic approach to his job. He wrote to M.C.C. warning them about the West Indian Charlie Griffith's action. 'Three kicks and yer out,' he would sometimes tell batsmen before the lbw law changed. The fearlessness may have been among the reasons he was never chosen for the Test panel, something that made him increasingly bitter; he never gave captains or top batsmen any special benefit of the doubt: 'I used to shoot 'em out, no matter who.' Lord's were also wary of the extent to which he fraternised with players.

Among the great Pepper stories is the one (which has many variations) about the mild-mannered League umpire who finally lost patience with his swearing appeals and shouted back: 'Not out, you fat Australian bastard.' He ended his own umpiring career just as helmets were coming in. When Dennis Amiss suggested Pepper might hold his, he replied: 'You hold it, mate, and use it as a pisspot.' On his death, one friend said Cec was the only man he knew who could talk, spit, chew, belch and pass wind simultaneously. Peter Wight, who umpired with him, said he listened as well as talked.

PICKLES, CANON HUGH JOHN, who died on September 24, 1989, aged 70, was a charming eccentric whose lifestyle suggested a character from *England, Their England*, rather than a modern clerk in Holy Orders. He declared that cricket became his second religion when he discovered the game on a day visit to The Oval, at the age of 12, to see the 1930 Australians. The England captain that day, R.E.S. Wyatt, sent a message of goodwill to a dinner held 50 years later to mark the occasion. A product of St Edward's School, Oxford, and University College, Hugh Pickles played most of his own enthusiastic cricket for clergy teams. He was captain/secretary of the Oxford Diocesan Clergy C.C. from 1964 to 1989, had captained Wantage after the war, and though very weak he had the immense pleasure of receiving the Church Times Cup on behalf of the Oxford Clergy when that team won the 1989 Diocesan final three weeks before his death. The previous season, his high-tossed, slow off-breaks had brought him a hat-trick, as much a delight to his friends as to himself. Parish priest at Blewbury for 26 years, he was indulged and loved by his parishioners, who became accustomed to his absence on cricketing matters: he was once given special leave by his Bishop to accompany Worcestershire to the West Indies in Holy Week as the county's honorary chaplain. Indeed, stories of cricketing enthusiasm diverting him from his other activities accompanied him all his life.

POOLEY, EDWARD, the once famous Surrey wicket-keeper, died in Lambeth Infirmary on July 18, 1907. He had for a long time been in very poor circumstances and was often compelled to seek the shelter of the workhouse. Born on February 13, 1838, he was in his 70th year. All through his cricket career it was generally supposed that he was born in 1843 and the real date of his birth was only made known by himself in his interview in *Old English Cricketers*. It seems that when he determined to take up cricket professionally his father thought that he would have a better chance if he knocked a few years off his age. Thus, though regarded at the time as quite a young player, he was over three and twenty when in May, 1861, he played at The Oval for a team of Surrey Colts against the Gentlemen of the Surrey Club with Hayes and Heartfield.

At the time his future fame as a wicket-keeper was unthought of, and presumably he was tried for his batting. Playing on the same side were Harry Jupp, and the still surviving J. Bristow. In 1862 Pooley was engaged as one of the bowlers at The Oval, but his regular connection with the Surrey XI did not begin until about 1865. In the meantime he played for Middlesex, making his first appearance at Lord's for that county against the M.C.C. on July 25, 1864. The match was a memorable one inasmuch as Grundy and Wootton got Middlesex out in the first innings for a total of 20.

The story of how he came to succeed Tom Lockyer is graphically told by himself in *Old English Cricketers*. He said: 'My introduction to wicket-keeping would be about the year 1863. Old Tom Lockyer's hands were bad, and the ground being fiery he could not take his usual place behind the sticks. Mr F.P. Miller, the Surrey captain, was in a quandary as to who should relieve him, so I, saucy-like, as usual, went up to him and said "Mr Miller, let me have a try." "You? What do you know about wicket-keeping? Have you ever kept wicket at all?" was Mr Miller's remark. "No, never, but I should like to try," I replied. "Nonsense" said he, and when just at that moment H.H. Stephenson came up and remarked "Let the young 'un have a go, sir," Mr Miller thereupon relented. I donned the gloves, quickly got two or three wickets, and seemed so much at home that Tom Lockyer was delighted, and said I was born to keep wicket and would have to be his successor in the Surrey team. What he said came true.'

In 1866, Pooley established his position as one of the leading professionals of the day and thenceforward he remained a member of the Surrey XI for 17 years, finally dropping out in 1883. His great days as a wicket-keeper date from the time of the late James Southerton's connection with Surrey in 1867. The two men helped each other enormously. Southerton's slow bowling with a pronounced off-break was then something comparatively new and while batsmen were learning to play him the wicket-keeper naturally had great chances. It is safe to say that no wicket-keeper then before the public could have assisted Southerton to the extent that Pooley did. He was quick as lightning and with all his brilliancy very safe. Partly from lack of opportunity he was not quite so good as Pinder or Tom Plumb to very fast bowling, but to slow bowling he was in his day supreme.

Two or three pages of *Wisden* could easily be filled with details of his doings, but it is sufficient to say here that the record of the greatest number of wickets obtained in a first-class match still stands to his credit after an interval of nearly 40 years. In the Surrey v. Sussex match at The Oval in July, 1868, he got rid of 12 batsmen, stumping one and catching five in the first innings and stumping three and catching three in the second. Curiously enough, Southerton was in the Sussex team in this match, players in those days being allowed to play for two counties in the same season if qualified by birth for one and by residence for the other. The rule was changed just afterwards and Southerton threw in his lot with Surrey.

Apart from his wicket-keeping Pooley was a first-rate bat, free in style, with fine driving power and any amount of confidence. He made many good scores and would without a doubt have been a much greater run-getter if he had not been so constantly troubled by damaged hands. During the Canterbury Week of 1871 he played an innings of 93 when suffering from a broken finger. Of the faults of private character that marred Pooley's career and were the cause of the poverty in which he spent the later years of his life there is no need now to speak. He was in many ways his own enemy, but even to the last he had a geniality and sense of humour that to a certain extent condoned his weaknesses.

POORE, EDWARD, who died after being bitten by a rat at Haifa, Israel, on June 29, 1991, aged 42, was a popular and eccentric spectator on the grounds of the county circuit. He spent his time at English cricket grounds when he was not roaming the world's trouble-spots. When he died, he was helping to run a hostel in the Arab quarter of Jerusalem. His ponytail and frequently bare feet successfully disguised the fact that he went to Harrow and was a great-nephew of Brigadier General R.M. Poore, who once scored 304 for Hampshire.

POORE, BRIG.-GEN. ROBERT MONTAGU, who during one season was the most prolific scorer in England, died on July 14, 1938, aged 72. He used to relate that he did not take seriously to cricket before going to India as a Lieutenant in the 7th Hussars. Then he studied textbooks on the game while playing in Army matches. From 1892 to 1895 when A.D.C. to Lord Harris, then Governor of Bombay, he averaged 80 for Government House. Going to South Africa, better opportunities came for finding his true ability when facing the formidable bowlers under the command of Lord Hawke. He hit up 112 at Pietermaritzburg and at Durban, when XV of Natal were set to get 228, he scored 107, being mainly responsible for the local side winning by five wickets; these were the only 100s scored against the touring team of 1895–96. He also appeared for South Africa in the three Test matches without distinguishing himself more than did some others in badly beaten XIs.

In the course of a few months in Natal he scored 1,600 runs, including nine separate 100s, so that when returning to England in 1898 at the age of 32, Major Poore was ready for first-class cricket. On a soft wicket at Lord's he scored 51 and helped appreciably in an innings victory for M.C.C. over Lancashire. He averaged 34 for 11 Hampshire matches and next season he became the most sensational batsman in the country, his doings being described as phenomenal. Making a late start he scored in two months – June 12 to August 12 – 1,399 runs for Hampshire with an average of 116.58. Major Poore hit seven centuries, two against Somerset at Portsmouth, and in his next innings another off the Lancashire bowlers at Southampton; he also scored exactly 100 runs in two innings against the Australians. In 21 first-class innings he made 1,551 runs, with an average of 91.23 – a figure not exceeded until Herbert Sutcliffe averaged 96.96 in 1931. The return with Somerset at Taunton was specially noteworthy, Major Poore scoring 304 and with captain E.G. Wynyard (225) adding 411 in four hours 20 minutes – the English record for the sixth wicket. Military duty took him back to South Africa before the end of the season, and after occasional appearances his county cricket ceased in 1906, but so well did he retain his form and activity that in 1923, when 57 years old, he hit three consecutive centuries during a tour of M.C.C. in the West Country.

A tall man at 6ft 4in, of massive frame with powerful limbs, Major Poore when at the top of his form used his long reach with great effect in driving, his strokes between the bowler and cover-point going with such speed over the turf that fieldsmen, no matter how placed, could not prevent him from scoring freely. Before becoming accustomed to English wickets, he played forward more in defence for smothering the ball than as a hitter, but his drive ripened to one of the most powerful ever known.

A versatile sportsman, Major Poore was one of the finest swordsmen in the Army, taking the highest honours at the Military Tournament. A first-rate polo player, he also twice won the West of India Lawn Tennis Championship, a feat he repeated in Matabeleland, and was in his regimental shooting team. His exceptional physical powers were demonstrated in his wonderful 1899 season; during a fortnight in June he played in the winning team of the Inter-Regimental Polo Tournament, won the best-man-at-arms mounted event at the Royal Naval and Military Tournament and scored three consecutive centuries for Hampshire, 104 and 119 not out against Somerset and 111 against Lancashire.

POWELL, ARCHIE, who died on December 27, 1963, aged 95, played for Gloucestershire Colts and, when catching W.G. Grace at cover-point, was reputed to be the only newspaperman ever to dismiss the Doctor for a duck. Powell contributed articles on cricket and rugby football to the *Daily Mail* for 40 years. A Bristol journalist, he was a director of the *Western Daily Press*.

PRICHARD, MAJOR HESKETH VERNON HESKETH, DSO, MC, FRGS, FZS, born in India on November 17, 1876, died at Gorhambury, near

St Albans, on June 14, 1922. He learned his cricket at Fettes and afterwards played successfully for Hampshire, M.C.C., the Gentlemen and other prominent teams. As a fast bowler he was most useful, his deliveries getting up very quickly from the pitch. For Hampshire he obtained 222 wickets for 23.11 runs each, and he was probably at his best in 1904 when, in all first-class matches, he took 106 wickets for an average of 21.92. He assisted the Gentlemen in 1903 and two following seasons, and took part in a couple of tours, visiting the West Indies with Lord Brackley in 1904–05 and America as a member of the M.C.C. team in 1907. When Kent were set 131 to win v. M.C.C. at Lord's in 1904, Hesketh Prichard took six wickets for 23 runs, the innings closing for 97. Half the side were out for 12, and he dismissed C.H.B. Marsham, Hardinge and Murrell without a run between them. He was well known as a traveller and author, and during the War carried out responsible duties and was twice Mentioned in Dispatches.

RAE, EDWARD, who introduced the game into Russian Lapland, died at Birkenhead on June 26, 1923, aged 76.

RATTIGAN, SIR TERENCE MERVYN, CBE, the famous playwriter, who died in Bermuda on November 30, 1977, aged 66, was, like his father and his uncle, in the Harrow XI. He won his place in 1929 as an opening bat, but next year though he played in the XI was not in the side at Lord's. He was an elegant stroke player, but unsound.

REES-DAVIES, WILLIAM RUPERT, QC, who died in January 1992, aged 75, was the outstanding public-school bowler in 1935 and the fastest seen at Eton since G.O.B. Allen. He took 34 wickets at 14.73, reserving his best form for the big occasions. In two games against Harrow and Winchester he had 14 victims and added a further 15 with impressive performances in the representative matches at Lord's. After such high promise, a Blue at Cambridge in 1936 seemed to be a certainty. But the burden of a reputation and the general air of expectancy undermined his confidence. He played seven matches but he was dogged by trouble with his inordinately long run-up. He did not turn out in 1937 and was fortunate to play at Lord's in 1938; Cambridge, with one of the weakest attacks for many years, had conceded a series of huge totals and he did not escape heavy punishment himself. In 15 first-class matches he captured 33 wickets at a cost of 43.42. His batting was negligible and he only managed 37 runs in 23 visits to the crease. Rees-Davies lost an arm in the war and afterwards was often in pain. He became a QC and was a Conservative MP for 30 years. He regularly pro-

posed measures to liberalise gambling and thus became known in the House, with varying degrees of affection, as 'the one-armed bandit'.

REMNANT, GEORGE HENRY, who died in February, 1941, aged 92, was the oldest living Kent professional cricketer and a friend of Charles Dickens. Born at Rochester on November 20, 1848, he made the first of 42 appearance for his county at the age of 20. His best score for Kent was 62 against Hampshire at Canterbury in 1877, but in minor cricket he hit 238 and 211 not out for Chilham Castle. He was a magnificent fieldsman. As a young man, Remnant played in the village team at Gad's Hill, Higham. He used to relate how, when playing in the meadow adjoining the house where Charles Dickens lived, he drove a ball into the back of a trap in which sat the novelist's children and their governess. The pony bolted; Remnant dropped his bat, dashed in pursuit, and checked the runaway before any harm could be done.

RICE, FATHER WILLIAM IGNATIUS, OSB, MA, who died at Douai Abbey on April 22, 1955, aged 72, was Headmaster of Douai School from 1915 to 1952. In his younger days he played for Warwickshire during the summer holidays and for some years enjoyed the distinction of being the only monk whose cricket performances were chronicled in *Wisden*.

ROBINSON, COMMANDER VIVIAN JOHN, RN (Retired), who died at Warminster on February 28, 1979, aged 81, was a member of the famous Backwell House family who for many years regularly produced their own XI, and a younger brother of D.C. Robinson, who captained Gloucestershire. A useful batsman and fast-medium bowler, he appeared for Gloucestershire against Oxford University in 1923.

ROSEBERY, SIXTH EARL OF, who died on May 30, 1974, aged 92, was a
cricketer, soldier, politician and administrator of distinction. When
Lord Dalmeny, he was in the Eton XI of 1900, scoring 52 against
Harrow and 55 against Winchester. In 1901 he turned out for
Buckinghamshire, took part in two matches for Middlesex the following season and began playing for Surrey in 1903. He took over
the Surrey captaincy in 1905 and held the post till 1907. Both his
centuries for the county were made at The Oval in 1905, against
Leicestershire and Warwickshire. While hitting the first, he drove
fiercely during a stand for the sixth wicket of 260 with J.N.
Crawford. That season was the first for Surrey of J.B. Hobbs, and
Lord Dalmeny was always proud of the fact that he awarded that
great batsman his cap after two games.

He succeeded to the title of Lord Rosebery when his father, a
former Prime Minister, died in 1929, and became President of
Surrey from 1947 to 1949. It was thanks to his approach to the
Prince of Wales in 1905 that the county club adopted the Prince of
Wales's feathers as their crest. For many years Lord Rosebery was a
celebrated figure in the world of horse racing. He left £9,650,986
net.

ROTHSCHILD, THE THIRD LORD (NATHANIEL MAYER VICTOR),
GBE, GM, FRS, who died in London on March 20, 1990, aged 79, was
one of the most versatile and gifted men of his time, and a cricketer
of considerable talent. In 1929, his last year at Harrow, he made his
mark in all departments of the game: he was one of three boys to
score more than 500 runs in schools matches, he took 20 wickets at
25 apiece, and he was a high-class performer in the slips. At Lord's
against Eton, opening with Terence Rattigan, he made a dashing 43
out of 68 to launch Harrow's reply to a total of 347, to which his
bizarre mixture of pace and spin had made much too generous a
contribution. He made runs for the Lord's Schools against the Rest,
and towards the end of August he was given a run by

Northamptonshire, making an auspicious start, including 36 against Larwood, Barrett and Voce after five wickets had gone down for 39. In 1930 he played in the Freshmen's match at Cambridge, and in a further trial he drove finely in making 112 for the Perambulators against the Etceteras. This innings and his highest first-class score of 63 against Kent at Peterborough (St Ames b Freeman) earned him a game for the University against Sussex. However, he found Maurice Tate too much of a handful in both innings. He was looked upon as a possible captain of Northamptonshire on the retirement of V.W.C. Jupp, but the job was given to W.C. Brown and Rothschild went on to conquer wider fields.

RUSHTON, WILLIAM GEORGE, who died on December 11, 1996, aged 59, was a well-known TV and radio humorist and a passionate follower of cricket. He regularly drew cartoons for *The Cricketer* – including the January 1997 cover illustration – and his novels included *W.G. Grace's Last Case*, a fantasy in which W.G. and Dr Watson foil a plot to take over the world by the Martians.

SALMON, ROSS OSBORNE SPENCER, DSC, who died on April 14, 2004, aged 81, was the Test match statistician for BBC TV from the mid-1960s until the early 1970s. If this implies dry meticulousness, it would be misleading. Salmon was an adventurer who led a life of astounding variety. He was a decorated wartime Navy pilot who flew secret missions deep into enemy territory (wearing a top hat and white gloves, apparently); he managed a ranch in Colombia until he broke 14 bones in a jungle air crash; and he became a children's TV star of the 1950s, as the Jungle Cowboy, in which guise he rode across Britain, turning up in school playgrounds complete with Stetson. He also set up his own ranch, the Lazy S, on the edge of Dartmoor but, after they were snowed in for three months during the winter of 1962–63, he took his family into Plymouth and concentrated on freelance journalism and broadcasting. Salmon took on the TV cricket job after a succession of previous incumbents had died young. It was not an obvious role for him: once his figures flew out of a train window. ('Can I have a pound of stats?' he asked Bill Frindall on arrival. 'Weight or value?' came the reply.) He was a silent, unseen presence for Test match viewers, but viewers in the South-West were familiar with his easy style, and colleagues were impressed by his ability to arrive breathless at the last minute, and still get things right. Salmon also started the International Crusaders, a charity team, and he had the knack of persuading stars like Garry Sobers and Fred Trueman to play for nothing.

SANDMAN, DONALD MCKAY, who died in Christchurch on January 29, 1973, aged 84, was one of New Zealand's most versatile sportsmen. As a good batsman and leg-break bowler, he played cricket for New Zealand in 1910, 1914 and 1921 and for 17 years assisted Canterbury in the Plunket Shield tournament. He was a half-back in the New Zealand Army rugby football team which toured South Africa in 1919 and turned out for South Island in 1921. He also excelled at billiards, hockey, badminton, boxing, lawn tennis, bowls and rifle shooting.

SATHASIVAM, MAHADEVAN, the most gifted and stylish batsman of Sri Lanka, died of a heart attack in 1977 at the age of 62 in Colombo. He made a style of his own and his stroke-play had perfect poise and power. Against Madras for Ceylon at the Chepauk Grounds, Madras, in 1947, he scored 215, a ground record until eclipsed by Joe Hardstaff (jnr) of Nottinghamshire fame several years later. Against Lala Amarnath's Indian team of 1945, he played a stylish innings of 111 at the Colombo Oval. Against the 1950 Commonwealth side led by L. Livingston, he made 98 at the Colombo Oval for Ceylon. He held the unique distinction of having captained three countries in cricket against visiting English and Australian teams – Sri Lanka, Singapore and Malaysia.

SELINCOURT, HUGH DE, author of many delightful books about cricket, died at his home near Pulborough, Sussex, on January 20, 1951. He was 72. Educated at Dulwich and University College, Oxford, Mr de Selincourt was for some years dramatic, then literary critic for London newspapers before he decided to devote his career to writing. Although his works were not confined to cricket, and there is no evidence that he was a specially accomplished player himself, he was perhaps best known for such tales as *The Cricket Match*, *Over* and *More Over*. These revealed particularly his love for cricket of the village-green variety.

SERJEANT, SIR DAVID MAURICE, MD, born at Ramsey, Hampshire, January 18, 1830, died at Camberwell, January 12, 1929, within a few days of entering upon his 100th year. As far back as August, 1850, he was a member of the XXII of Peterborough side which beat the All England XI by 13 wickets. In that game he scored five and five, being caught by Felix off Martingell in the first innings and bowled by Wisden in the second. Clarke, Hillyer and Alfred Mynn also bowled. Going to Australia whilst still a young man, Sir David opened the innings for Victoria in each of the two matches ever played against New South Wales – at Melbourne in March, 1856, and at Sydney in January, 1857. To the end of his long life he took the deepest interest in cricket, and as recently as 1926 was among those who welcomed the Australians on their arrival in London. He was the author of *Australia: Its Cricket Bat, Its Kangaroo, Its Farming, Fruit and Flowers*.

SIDNEY, THOMAS STAFFORD, KC, Attorney-General, Leeward Islands. Died in Liverpool November 16, 1917, aged 54. Author of *'W.G.' up to date*, published at Ootacamund in 1896. Member of M.C.C. since 1888.

SILKIN, LORD OF DULWICH, PC, QC, died on August 17, 1988, aged 70. A useful schoolboy cricketer, especially as a bowler of leg-breaks, Samuel Charles Silkin captained Dulwich in 1936 before going up to Cambridge later that year. He had little success in the Freshmen's match in 1937 and although given further trials in 1938, including a match for the University against the Army, he did not win a Blue. Eligible for Glamorgan, having been born at Neath, he was invited to play for the county when Cambridge visited on tour later in the season but again he achieved little. These two first-class appearances resulted in four runs and two wickets, and from then his cricket was mostly at club level, with some appearances for the Glamorgan and Middlesex Second XIs. Elected as Member of Parliament for

Camberwell in 1964, he held the seat for Labour until his retirement in 1983 and was Attorney General from 1974 to 1979. He was made a life peer in 1985.

SKELDING, ALEXANDER, who died at Leicester on April 17, 1960, aged 73, stood as a first-class umpire from 1931 to 1958. He began his cricket career as a very fast bowler with Leicestershire in 1905, but, because he wore spectacles, was not re-engaged at the end of the season. He then joined Kidderminster in the Birmingham League and achieved such success that in 1912 the county re-signed him and he continued with them till 1929. His best season was that of 1927, when he took 102 wickets, average 20.81. Altogether he dismissed 593 batsmen at a cost of less than 25 runs each. One of the most popular personalities in the game, he always wore white boots when umpiring and he was celebrated for his sense of humour. It was his custom at the close of play to remove the bails with an exaggerated flourish and announce: 'And that concludes the entertainment for the day, gentlemen.'

Alec was the central figure in many amusing incidents. Once in response to an appeal for a run out, he stated: 'That was a "photo-finish" and as there isn't time to develop the plate, I shall say not out.' In another match a batsman who had been celebrating a special event the previous evening was rapped on the pad by a ball. At once the bowler asked: 'How is he?' Said Alec, shaking his head sadly: 'He's not at all well, and he was even worse last night.' Occasionally the joke went against Alec. In a game in 1948 he turned down a strong appeal by the Australian touring team. A little later a dog ran on to the field, and one of the Australians captured it, carried it to Skelding and said: 'Here you are. All you want now is a white stick!' Asked in his playing days if he found spectacles a handicap, Alec said: 'The specs are for the look of the thing. I can't see without 'em and on hot days I can't see with 'em, because they get steamed up. So I bowl on hearing only and appeal twice an over.'

One of his most cherished umpiring memories was the giving of three leg-before decisions which enabled H. Fisher of Yorkshire to perform a unique hat-trick against Somerset at Sheffield in 1932. 'I was never more sure that I was right in each case,' he said afterwards, 'and each of the batsmen agreed that he was dead in front.'

SMITH, ARTHUR, who died on October 18, 1991, aged 79, sold score-cards and newspapers on Yorkshire grounds for more than 50 years. He was a much-loved institution at Headingley, where his gravelly voice shouting 'Up-to-date scorecards' or 'Green Final' was the inevitable background accompaniment to every great moment on the field.

SMITH, SIR CHARLES AUBREY, CBE, famous in the world of cricket before making a name on the stage and becoming a universal favourite on the films in comparatively recent years, died on December 20, 1948, aged 85, at Beverly Hills, California. Born in London on July 21, 1863, the son of a doctor, C.A. Smith went to Charterhouse School and bowled with such success that it came as no surprise that he gained his Blue at Cambridge when a Freshman in 1882.

Four times he played at Lord's against Oxford and, by a remark-able series of coincidences, all of these matches ended with a decisive margin of seven wickets, Cambridge winning three of these interesting encounters. In the 1884 match which Oxford won, C.A. Smith was not out 0 in each innings and took two wickets for 65 runs, but in the other three games he showed his worth. In 1883 he helped C.T. Studd dismiss Oxford for 55 and in the second innings he took six wickets for 78 and Oxford just equalled the Cambridge total 215. He made four catches in the match. His last effort for the Light Blues brought six wickets for 81. His captains were the three brothers Studd and the Hon. M.B. Hawke.

He played for Sussex from 1882 until 1896, with varying regularity, and was captain from 1887 to 1889. For Gentlemen at Lord's in 1888 he and S.M.J. Woods dismissed the last four players for one run scored after A.G. Steel handed the ball to Smith. In the match Woods took ten wickets for 76 and C.A. Smith five for 36.

In the previous winter he went to Australia, captaining the side organised by Shaw and Shrewsbury and in 1888–89 he captained the first English side which went to South Africa. Major R.G. Warton, the Australian, was manager. All the matches were against 'odds' except two engagements called 'English Team v. XI of South Africa,' but some years afterwards given the description 'Tests.' During the tour C.A. Smith took 134 wickets at 7.61 each, a modest achievement compared with the 290 wickets at 5.62 credited to John Briggs, the Lancashire left-hander.

Smith stayed in South Africa for a time in partnership with M.P. Bowden, of Surrey, a member of the team, as stockbrokers. During this period he captained Transvaal against Kimberley in the first Currie Cup match in April 1890, so initiating a competition which has done much to raise the standard of cricket in South Africa. Among C.A. Smith's best bowling performances were five wickets for eight runs for Sussex against The University at Cambridge in 1885, and seven for 16 against M.C.C. at Lord's in 1890. A hard-hitting batsman, he scored 142 for Sussex at Hove against Hampshire in 1888. Over six feet tall, he made an unusual run-up to deliver the ball and so became known as 'Round The Corner' Smith. Sometimes he started from a deep mid-off position, at others from behind the umpire, and, as described by W.G. Grace, 'it is rather startling when he suddenly appears at the bowling crease.'

He maintained his love for cricket to the end. Until a few years ago he captained the Hollywood side and visited England for the Test matches, the last time as recently as 1947, when South Africa

were here. He was knighted in 1944 in recognition of his support of Anglo-American friendship. A very good Association outside-right, he played for Old Carthusians and Corinthians.

SMITHSON, GERALD A., who died suddenly on September 6, 1970, aged 43, played for Yorkshire in 1946 and 1947, his highest innings for the county being 169 against Leicestershire at Leicester in the second year. Conscripted as a Bevin Boy in the mines after the war, he received special permission, after his case had been debated in the House of Commons, to tour the West Indies with the M.C.C. team of 1947–48, taking part in two Test matches. His picture appeared in *Wisden* 1948, page 38. In 1951 he joined Leicestershire, with whom he remained for six seasons, of which his best was that of 1952 when, by attractive left-hand batting and the aid of two centuries, he hit 1,264 runs, average 28.08. He afterwards served as coach, first at Caterham School and then at Abingdon School, and between 1957 and 1962 he also assisted Hertfordshire.

SOPER, REV. BARON, died on December 22, 1998, aged 95. Donald Soper was a Methodist preacher and orator of enormous power, a staunch pacifist, and one of Britain's most famous 20th-century churchmen. As a schoolboy, at Aske's, Hatcham, just after the First World War, he was a bowler of considerable pace. In a school match, a ball bowled by Soper bounced and hit the batsman over the heart. The boy died. William Purcell wrote in *A Portrait of Soper*: 'The degree to which this upset Donald at the time and the persistence of the memory of it – he was recalling it 50 years later – suggest an abhorrence of violence which was possibly an unconscious ingredient of his later pacifism.'

SOYRES, REV. JOHN DE, Rector of St John the Evangelist's, St John's, New Brunswick, who died suddenly on February 3, 1905, while undergoing an operation, was a great lover of cricket. He was born

in Somerset in 1849, and educated at Brighton College and at Gonville and Caius College, Cambridge, where he had a most distinguished career. He went out to New Brunswick in 1888, and had made for himself a reputation as the most distinguished preacher in Eastern Canada. He was a nephew of Edward Fitzgerald, the translator of Omar Khayyam.

SPALDING, ALBERT GOODWILL, born at Byron, Illinois, on September 2, 1850, died at Point Loma, California, on September 9, 1915. A famous baseballer, he brought a team to England in 1874 which played seven cricket matches, winning four and drawing three. In the early 1880s he was a member of the Chicago C.C. XI. He was the head of a well-known American sporting outfitter's firm bearing his name.

SPRING, LEICESTER RUSSELL, who died on May 31, 1997, aged 88, was a fast-medium bowler who played three matches for Auckland in 1936–37 and twice dismissed Walter Hadlee. He founded the *Whakatane Beacon* newspaper and by 1953 was able to buy his first racehorse, Rising Fast, which won nine races out of 11, including the Melbourne Cup.

SPROT, CAPT. EDWARD MARK, an all-round sportsman of much ability, died on October 8, 1945, at his home at Farnham, Surrey, aged 75. Born in Scotland and educated at Harrow, he made a name in Army cricket before playing first for Hampshire in 1898 and in company with many noted soldiers (among them Captain E.G. Wynyard, Major R.M. Poore, Colonel J.G. Greig – giving their rank at that time), he helped to raise Hampshire to such a good standard that during his captaincy they reached fifth place in the county championship. He held the reins from 1903 until 1914, and under his lead Hampshire invariably played attractive cricket with enterprise and enthusiasm. Himself a fine free hitter with zest for the forcing game, Captain Sprot, for a man of medium physique, put plenty of power into his strokes, made in free style that meant quick run-getting when he was at the crease.

In first-class cricket he scored 12,251 runs, including 13 hundreds, averaging 28.55 an innings, and with slowish bowling took 54 wickets, besides holding 208 catches. Clearly a valuable man for any county, and as captain in 1918 at Southampton he aroused admiration and astonishment by declaring the innings closed when Hampshire, with a wicket to fall, were 24 behind their visitors, Northamptonshire, at lunch time on the third day, after rain had hindered the progress of the match. By this action he saved the interval between the innings and he soon put on Phillip Mead, little known as a bowler. Six wickets for 18 runs fell to Mead's left-hand slows. Hampshire wanted no more than 86 runs for victory and when A. C. Johnston was out at three, Sprot hit up 62 in less than an hour, two sixes and eight fours being characteristic of his determined aggression. Alec Bowell was the watchful partner in gaining a victory which *Wisden* described as without parallel, which makes a unique incident in the history of the game. Sprot saw the possibility of victory by dismissing the opposition on a drying pitch and went for runs with the success described – a splendid example of dynamic cricket which Sir Stanley Jackson's Committee has asked for in first-class cricket of the future.

When serving with the Shropshire Light Infantry in 1899 Sprot, with Colonel J. Spens, won The Army Racquets Challenge Cup. An admirable golf player, a sure shot and clever fisherman, Sprot found billiards the most fascinating indoor recreation, and on a strange table in Cairo he won a 200-up game from the opening left by his opponent on starting the play.

STUDD, CHARLES THOMAS, the youngest and most famous of three brothers, all of whom played for Eton, Cambridge University and

Middlesex, was born at Spatton, Northants., on December 2, 1860, and died at Ibambi in the Belgian Congo on July 16, 1931. Each of the three brothers enjoyed the distinction of captaining the Cambridge XI – G.B. in 1882, C.T. in 1883 and J.E.K. in 1884. J.E.K., the eldest – Lord Mayor of London in 1929 – left Eton in 1877 but did not go up to Cambridge until 1881. All three figured in the Eton XI of 1877 and also in the Cambridge XIs of 1881 and 1882.

A great batsman, a fine field and a high-class bowler, C.T. Studd developed his powers so rapidly that, whilst still at Cambridge, he was in the best XI of England. He possessed a fine upright style in batting and was particularly strong on the off-side. He bowled right-hand rather above medium pace and, tall of build, brought the ball over from a good height.

In 1882 he made 118 for Cambridge University and 114 for the M.C.C. against probably the strongest bowling Australia ever sent to this country, the side including, as it did, Spofforth, Palmer, Boyle, Garrett and Giffen. That year he also scored 100 at Lord's for Gentlemen against Players, yet he finished the season ingloriously at Kennington Oval with the memorable match which England lost by seven runs. Bowled by Spofforth in the first innings without scoring he, in the second innings, despite the two hundreds he had hit against the Australians earlier in the summer, went in tenth and, when the end came just afterwards, was not out 0. He was a member of the team taken out to Australia in the winter of 1882–83 by the Hon. Ivo Bligh. This side, if beaten by Australia, won two matches out of three against the men who had visited England in the previous summer and so were acclaimed as having brought back The Ashes.

Unhappily for English cricket C.T. Studd was not seen in the field after 1884. Feeling a call for missionary work, he went out to China in connection with the China Inland Mission and there remained from 1885 to 1895. Invalided home, he engaged in missionary work in England and America and after 1900 with the

Anglo-Indian Evangelization Society. Later on the state of the multitudes of the Belgian Congo, which had not been touched by any missionary agency, made such strong appeal to him that he went out to that uncivilised region and, despite numerous illnesses and many hardships, devoted the remainder of his life to missionary work there.

TAYLOR, DR CLIFFORD JOHN, FRCS, LSA, who died at Chatham after a long illness on November 10, 1952, aged 76, played in a few matches for Gloucestershire at the end of the 19th century. He liked to relate how, in 1899, when he dismissed K.S. Ranjitsinhji in a match against Sussex, the famous batsman called to him: 'Well bowled, young 'un!' After qualifying at Edinburgh University, Taylor practised medicine in London and Chelmsford before going to Chatham in 1910. In the First World War he served with the R.A.M.C. in Egypt and Palestine.

THOMS, ROBERT. For some time before he passed away on June 10, 1903, there had been such very bad accounts for Bob Thoms' health that no one was at all surprised when the announcement of his death appeared in the papers. It had been known for some months there was no chance of his recovery, but less than two months before his death he had so much to say about cricket and his mind was still so bright that it did not seem as if the end were quite so near. He broke up very rapidly at the finish, and died after one final rally. In him there has gone a remarkable and interesting personality.

No one had a more thorough knowledge of cricket, or could speak with greater authority about all the leading players of the last 60 years. Ambitious of being a public cricketer himself, he came out at Lord's when Fuller Pilch was the best bat in England, and it was his privilege to watch the triumphs of George Parr, Hayward, Carpenter, Richard Daft, Jupp, Tom Humphrey, E.M. Grace, W.G. Grace, and all the other great run-getters down to Ranjitsinhji and C.B. Fry. Even in the season of 1902 he saw Victor Trumper bat at the Hastings Festival, and complimented him on his splendid innings of 120 against the South of England. Thoms always looked at cricket with the eyes of a young man, and was quite free from the fault – so common among men who live to a great age – of thinking that all the good things belonged to the past.

To Middlesex cricket, with which he was closely associated from the formation of the county club in the sixties, he was always devoted, and nothing cheered him up more in his last illness than visits from Mr V.E. Walker and Mr A.J. Webbe. He was never tired of referring to the Middlesex XI in the days when V.E. Walker was captain, and was very proud of the fact that he stood umpire in every first-class match played on the old Cattle Market ground at Islington. Right up to the end he had a singularly retentive memory, and when in congenial company he would tell numberless stories about the Walkers, C.F. Buller, and A.W.T. Daniel. In those distant days, of course, the modern system had not been adopted, and each county always appointed its own umpire.

The Graces, as cricketers, had no more fervent admirer than Thoms, and he was fond of saying that if W.G. Grace had not been such a marvellous bat he would have been the best slow bowler in England, his head work being so remarkable and his command of length so perfect. Of E.M. Grace's all-round capabilities, too, and especially his fielding at point, Thoms would never weary of talking. Among modern bowlers he, in common with most good judges, placed Spofforth first, while fully recognising the great qualities of Palmer, Turner and George Lohmann. As to the bowlers of his younger days, he thought very highly indeed of Hillyer and John Wisden. Curiously enough the present writer never heard him speak of Buttress, the famous but unfortunately too thirsty leg-breaker, who has been described by more than one distinguished cricketer of the past as absolutely the most difficult bowler England ever produced. Buttress's sovereign gift was his power of bowling a deadly leg-break with a real control over his pitch. He got so much spin on the ball that, according to Mr Henry Perkins, the man who tried to play him without gloves on was almost certain to have the skin knocked off his knuckles.

In dress, manner and appearance Thoms belonged essentially to the sixties, looking exactly like the photographs of some of the players of those days. He had a keen sense of humour, and told his cricket stories in a short, crisp way peculiarly his own. It was to be regretted that he did not, during the throwing controversy, bring the weight of his authority to bear on the side of fair bowling, but the traditions of his youth were too strong for him, and he always shrank from the task. However, in a quiet way he made his influence felt, plainly telling the leading amateurs that if they wanted to rid the game of an evil they all admitted they must act for themselves and not throw the whole onus on the umpires. Moreover, he was the means of some audacious young throwers dropping out of county cricket, his kindly method being to get them employment in other directions.

Though cricket was the main interest of his life Thoms was a good all-round sportsman, taking as a young man a keen delight in foot racing and the prize ring. He was a good runner himself, and could, so it is said, do a hundred yards in ten and a half seconds. Of anything he took up he was bound to be a good judge, his perception of excellence amounting to an absolute gift. He often talked about putting into book form his 60 years' experience of the cricket field, but whether he ever seriously commenced the task one cannot say.

TINDALL, THE REV. HENRY CHARLES LENOX, a great runner and well-known cricketer, died on June 11, 1940, at Peasmarsh, Sussex, aged 77. Although a good all-round cricketer – useful bat with sound style, fast bowler and dashing fieldsman – Tindall failed to get his Blue at Cambridge at a time when University cricket was very strong. He appeared occasionally for Kent without doing much, but was prominent in Sussex club cricket. Among many good performances, especially for South Saxons, he took all 10 wickets at a cost of only 25 runs for Hastings Rovers against Rye in 1906. In the Hastings Festival of 1894 he appeared for Gentlemen against Players. He set up a quarter-mile record in 1889 by winning the Amateur Championship in 48½ seconds, and also won the half-mile in one minute 56 seconds. In 1886 he won the 100 yards and quarter-mile in the University sports, and for several years was prominent at all distances from 100 to 1,000 yards. At the private schools at Hurst Court, Ore, and High Croft he found many cricketers of promise. An originator of the Rye Golf Club, he became chairman of the committee.

TINNISWOOD, PETER, who died of cancer on January 9, 2003, aged 66, was a prolific and original comic writer with an eye for the minutiae of English life. His genre was initially abrasive northern surrealism, but in the 1980s he turned his attention to cricket and through one character, a crusty cricket obsessive known as the Brigadier, created *Tales from a Long Room*, a fantasy on 'our summer game' riddled with puns, verbal abuse and whimsical name-play. It began as a radio monologue with Robin Bailey, who had played Uncle Mort in Tinniswood's television masterpiece *I Didn't Know You Cared*, as the Brigadier, recalling the M.C.C. tour of the Belgian Congo in 1914: 'There were at least two outbreaks of cannibalism among spectators . . . which I am convinced were responsible for the loss of our most promising young leg-spinner, M. M. Rudman-Stott. He was sent out to field at deep third man in the match against an Arab Slavers' Country XI, and all we found of him after the tea interval was the peak of his Harlequins cap and half an indelible pencil.'

In time, Tinniswood transported listeners to the snug hamlet of Witney Scrotum, introducing them to Granny Roebuck who ran the cake shop, Mr Bruce Woodcock of *The Times*, E.W. 'Gloria' Swanton, Winston Place, the former Lancashire batsman and one of Tinniswood's real-life heroes, and the recurrent Mr H.D. 'Dickie'

Bird. There was also romance. 'Into my view she glided; a tall, slim sylphlike figure in purest white. My heart missed a beat. The sap rose in my loins. Dear God, she was the spitting image of Herbert Sutcliffe. Call it the impetuosity of youth if you will, but remember I had been out of the country for many years, serving my King and country in some of the remotest and most primitive outposts of his Empire. I had not seen a first-class cricketer for seven years.'

The monologues spawned several books, a stage play with Willie Rushton as the Brigadier, recalling army times in the Far East and the massive earthworks at Botham's Gut, a column in *The Cricketer*, even a shortlived television version. Though seriously ill, and able to communicate only through an electronic voicebox, Tinniswood continued to write prodigiously and was *Wisden's* book reviewer in 2000.

TITLEY, UEL ADDISON, who died on November 11, 1973, aged 67, appeared for the XI while at Rugby, but did not get his colours. He went up to Cambridge and for some years afterwards held an appointment in Brazil. He wrote on cricket for some years for *The Times*, but was better known as the rugby correspondent for that newspaper. His excellent style and occasional flashes of humour earned him great respect in the football world, but his biggest achievement was the compilation of the *History of the Rugby Football Union* published in their centenary year, 1971. His unusual first name was given by his father, Samuel Titley, who said: 'Everybody calls me Sam. The boy can have the other half.'

TOZER, DR C.J., who died in Sydney on December 21, 1920, was one of the best of the younger generation of Australian batsmen. For New South Wales Colts against those of Victoria in 1912–13 he scored 83, 80 and 63, and in the same season made 78 not out v. Queensland and 54 v. West Australia. In the season before his death he scored 51 and 103 for New South Wales against Queensland at Brisbane.

TRYON, Lieut., of the Grenadier Guards, died in South Africa, from enteric fever, in the third week of April, 1901. He played occasionally for Northamptonshire in 1898, making 61 against the Surrey Second XI. He was a nephew of the late Sir George Tryon, who went down in the *Victoria*, off Tripoli, in June, 1892. He was born on October 22, 1878, and was thus only in his 23rd year at the time of his death.

TUCKER, WILLIAM ELDON, CVO, MBE, TD, FRCS, who died at his home in Bermuda on August 4, 1991, aged 87, was a distinguished orthopaedic surgeon, who chose to specialise in sporting injuries. The cricket-loving public and especially admirers of Denis Compton may not have realised that the extension of his career beyond 1949 until 1957 was entirely due to Tucker, who performed a series of operations on the most celebrated knee in the land. Tucker himself was a sportsman, who played rugby for England, winning three caps.

TWISTLETON-WYKEHAM-FIENNES, REV. THE HON. WINFIELD STRATFORD, born at Adlestrop, in Gloucestershire, on May 1, 1834, died at Broughton Castle, Banbury, on October 10, 1923, in his 90th year. He was the fourth son of Frederick, 16th Baron Saye and Sele. *Scores and Biographies* (4-289) said of him: 'Is a sharp quick hitter and bowls round-armed of a moderate speed with a pretty delivery.' In his four Public School matches for Winchester in 1851 and 1852 against Harrow and Eton he made 63 runs in eight innings and took 15 wickets. Obtaining his Blue for Oxford in 1856, he appeared three times against Cambridge, scoring 47 runs in five innings and taking 14 wickets. In another match at Liverpool he took five wickets with consecutive balls. His county cricket was played for Herefordshire and Oxfordshire. His elder brother, Mr C.B., was also in the XI whilst at Winchester.

W

WALKER, REV. JOHN SPENCER MULLINS, who died at Hove on November 19, 1953, in his 101st year, played in the Lancing cricket XIs of 1870 to 1872 and in the Association football teams of 1867 to 1872. Known as The Father of Sussex Football, he was one of a committee of three boys who in 1871 gave the Association code a trial in place of a game played only at Lancing. He was the oldest living old boy of the school. He played for Clapham Rovers in the F.A. Cup semi-final at Kennington Oval in 1874, when four spectators saw the victory of Oxford University by 1-0, and he became the first President of the Sussex F.A. in 1881. For 13 years after graduating at Oxford he was assistant master at Lancing, and later spent 30 years as Vicar of Amport St Mary, Hampshire, before retiring to Hove in 1935.

WALSINGHAM, BARON – in his cricket days the Hon. T. de Grey – died on December 3, 1919, in his 77th year. He was born in London on July 29, 1843. Though he played for Norfolk as late as 1868, he did not keep up his cricket very seriously after his University days. He was in the Eton XI in 1860 and 1861, and though overshadowed by R.A.H. Mitchell in both years and by the Hon. C.J. Lyttelton (now Lord Cobham) in 1860, he was one of the school's trusted batsmen, always going in first. In the big school matches he was never on the losing side, Eton beating Winchester in both his years, and drawing both games with Harrow at Lord's. I learn from the late Mr W.J. Ford's book that he had an excellent record as a batsman for Cambridge, his averages for four years being 32, 22, 24, and 17. Sir Henry Plowden says of him in Mr Ford's book: "Tommy de Grey, now Lord Walsingham, was among the finest fields of the day, especially at cover-point. As a batsman he had as much confidence as any one. His defence was very strong; his amusement to have two or three bowlers going at once in practice, with a fourth stump on the off side to encourage them.' In 1863 the Hon. T. de Grey had the honour of being chosen for Gentlemen v. Players at Lord's, but Tarrant and Jackson were a little too good for him; he was bowled for two and eight.

Apart from cricket he was at one time the best game shot in England. His record of 1,070 grouse to his own gun in one day in August, 1888, has, I believe, never been equalled. He was still more famous for his wonderful collection – by far the finest in the world – of micro-lepidoptera (the smaller butterflies and moths). He presented the whole collection in 1910 to the Natural History Museum at South Kensington.

WARD, THOMAS ALFRED, the South African wicket-keeper, was accidentally electrocuted when working at the West Springs Gold Mine on February 16, 1936. He came to England in 1912 and 1924 and if not so brilliant as Halliwell and Sherwell, who preceded him, or Cameron, he maintained a high standard of excellence. During that period he kept wicket in 23 Test matches, the first being at Old Trafford against Australia in the triangular tournament, and was thoroughly reliable. A dogged batsman with strong defence, he scored in Test cricket 459 runs with an average of 13.90. Going in first, he made 64 at Johannesburg in February, 1923, against the England side captained by F.T. Mann, and in 1924 at Old Trafford he again opened the innings well by scoring 50. When the Australian Imperial Forces team visited South Africa on the way home in 1919 Ward scored 62 not out at Johannesburg in the first of two representative games. He was in the Transvaal XI from 1909 to 1927, and in all first-class matches scored 1,651 runs with an average of 15.43. Born on August 2, 1887 he died in his 49th year.

WARDILL, MAJOR BENJAMIN JOHNSON, born at Everton, Liverpool, October 15, 1842; died at Melbourne, October 17, 1917. Secretary to Melbourne C.C., 1878 to 1910, when he retired owing to ill health; in 1878 there were only 400 members, but in 1910 between 5,000 and 6,000. He was Manager of the Australian teams in England in 1886, 1899, and 1902. He went to Australia at the age of 19, and in his young days was a useful cricketer. He did much to popularise rifle shooting in Australia, and was himself a splendid shot. Was one of the Victorians who visited Wimbledon in 1876 on their way to compete at the first Rifle Competition at Creedmore, U.S.A., during the Philadelphia Exhibition. Major Wardill was very fond of England, and came here more than once on visits after the tour of 1902. As manager for the Australians he had rather a trying experience in 1886, when the players did not get on well together, but he thoroughly enjoyed his subsequent trips.

WARDINGTON, The Second Baron, died on July 6, 2005, aged 81. The Hon. Christopher Henry Beaumont 'Bic' Pease, as he was known before succeeding to the title, opened the batting for Eton in 1941 and 1942, when he scored a match-winning 43 not out against Harrow. He later became one of Britain's leading bibliophiles, amassing the country's largest private collection of atlases at Wardington Manor, Oxfordshire.

WATSON, HAROLD, who died on March 14, 1969, aged 81, played as a professional fast-medium bowler for Norfolk before and after the First World War. Making his first appearance in 1910, he altogether took 384 wickets, average 17.23. On the ground staff at Lord's, he played for M.C.C. and in 1913 enjoyed the distinction of bowling F.E. Woolley, the great Kent and England left-hand batsman, with his first delivery in first-class cricket. Watson was also a useful hard-hitting batsman. He was at one time coach at the R.N.C. Dartmouth, Bishop's Stortford College and Perse School and later served as head porter at Trinity College, Cambridge.

WAUGH, ALEC, brother of Evelyn, died in Florida on September 3, 1981, aged 83. A great lover of cricket, he was Bobby Southcott in A.G. Macdonell's *England, Their England*, and for 50 years seldom missed a Test match at Lord's.

WEBBER, LIEUT. HENRY (South Lancashire Regiment), of Horley, Surrey, and a JP for the county, was killed in action on July 21, 1916, aged 68. He was in the Tonbridge School XI 50 years before, among his contemporaries being Mr J.W. Dale, and later played for Pembroke College, Oxford. He had been a member of the M.C.C. since 1872. He made his first hundred in 1863 and as recently as August 6, 1904, when 56 years of age, made 209 not out for Horley v. Lowfield Heath, at Horley, in three hours after a full round of golf in the morning. His pluck and patriotism in insisting on being given a commission at his advanced age were much admired.

WEST, WILLIAM ARTHUR JOHN, a popular member of the ground staff at Lord's for many years and a first-class umpire, sometimes 'standing' in Test matches, died on February 22, 1938, aged 75. After playing as an amateur for Northamptonshire, he turned professional in 1886 and was engaged at The Oval for two seasons. Then he joined the M.C.C. staff and continued to assist Northamptonshire until 1891 when he helped Warwickshire, the county of his birth, his best performance with the ball being five wickets for seven runs against Cheshire. All these counties were at that time second-class. Over 6ft tall and powerfully built, 'Bill' West was a fast bowler and hard hitter. In the 1880s he excelled as an amateur boxer, winning the Queensberry Cup in 1884, and next year the Amateur Boxing Association heavyweight cup.

WHEAT, ARTHUR B., who died on May 20, 1973, aged 75, was occasioned with Nottinghamshire County cricket for over half a century, first as wicket-keeper and then as scorer. He joined the staff in 1922 after gaining something of a reputation in the Notts and Derby League with Jacksdale who, during his three seasons with them, won the Championship three times and the Cup twice. He was first choice for Nottinghamshire during the heyday of that celebrated pair of fast bowlers, Larwood and Voce. When his playing career ended in 1947, he became county scorer and held the position for 26 years, in which time he scored for England in every Test match at Trent Bridge. He was the longest serving scorer for a first-class county. This likeable little man went into the mines upon leaving school, spent most of the Second World War years in that occupation and returned underground every winter. In 1972 he received a presentation to mark his 50 years' service to the County Club.

WHITEHEAD, LIEUT. GEORGE WILLIAM EDENDALE (RFA, ATTACHED RAF), born 1895, killed on October 17, 1918. Among the many public-school cricketers lost during the war perhaps none, except John Howell of Repton, had better prospects of winning distinction at the game than George Whitehead. In the Clifton College XI for four years – he was captain in 1913 and 1914 – he had a brilliant record at school. Starting in 1911, he was third in batting with an average of 33, and in the following year he did still better, playing a remarkable innings of 259 not out against Liverpool and averaging 41. Moreover he took 14 wickets with a fairly good average. Against Cheltenham he played a first innings of 63. In his two years as captain he was conspicuously successful, heading the batting in both seasons with averages of 46 in 1913 and 40 in 1914. He also bowled well, especially in 1914, when he took 36 wickets for a trifle over 13 runs apiece. He played three times at Lord's for Public Schools against the M.C.C., and in 1914 he was given a couple of trials for Kent.

An old Cliftonian writes: 'George Whitehead was a perfect flower of the public schools. He was not limited to athletics only, great though he was in this respect. Intellectually he was far above the average, and was as happy with a good book as when he was scoring centuries. His ideals were singularly high and though gentle and broad-minded, he always stood uncompromisingly for all that was clean. So modest was he that strangers sometimes failed to realize his worth. He insisted on being transferred to the Royal Air Force from the R.F.A., fully appreciating the risks, because he knew of his country's then urgent need of air-men and so he died, greatly patriotic. Clifton has lost more than 500 of her sons in the war. She is proud of every one of them, but of none more than of this very perfect gentleman.'

WHYSALL, WILLIAM WILFRID, who had reached the height of his fame last season, died in hospital at Nottingham on November 11, 1930. About a fortnight earlier he had fallen on a dance floor and injured his elbow. Septicaemia set in and, although a blood transfusion was performed, he passed away. Born at Woodborough, Notts, on October 31, 1887, he was only 43 years of age at the time of his death. He matured slowly as a cricketer, and not until 1908 was he invited to join the ground staff at Trent Bridge. Two seasons later he made 140 for Notts 2nd XI at Trent Bridge against Staffordshire, who had Sydney Barnes to bowl for them.

While a useful wicket-keeper, he played for the county as a batsman and, though first tried for Nottinghamshire in 1910, he did not realize expectations until ten years later when, after the long break due to the War, he resumed his place in the side. From that time he forged ahead rapidly until he became the most reliable batsman in the XI, a position he held unchallenged last summer when he headed the averages with 47.84 for an aggregate of 1,866. During five consecutive summers he had an aggregate of over 2,000 runs in first-class matches and in 1929 he made 2,716 runs.

Whysall possessed unlimited patience and a defence most difficult to penetrate. He could bring off all the strokes known to a
modern batsman and, when really set, his pulling and off-driving
were very sure. During the summer of 1921 Whysall became the rec-
ognized opening batsman with George Gunn and, altogether, the
pair took part in 40 first-wicket three-figure stands for the county.
He was a capable catch in the slips. On the strength of his ability as
a wicket-keeper as well as a batsman, he secured a place as deputy
to Strudwick in the M.C.C. team that toured Australia under the
captaincy of A.E.R. Gilligan in the winter of 1924–25, but it was for
his batting that he played in three of the Test Matches, scoring 186
runs with an average of 37.20. When England lost the third Test
Match by 11 runs, he was the highest scorer with 75 in the great
effort to gain a victory.

WILKINSON, COL. WILLIAM ALEXANDER CAMAC, DSO, MC, GM, who
died at Storrington on September 19, 1983, aged 90, was a soldier of
great gallantry in two wars and a cricketer who overcame a serious
handicap to become one of the most consistent batsmen of his day
in a high class of club cricket and indeed, when the opportunity
offered, in first-class cricket. A legendary character whose outspo-
kenness knew no close season, he was no respecter of persons; yet
he is seldom mentioned by anyone who knew him without genuine
affection. Leaving Eton too young to have been in the XI and finishing his school education in Australia, where his father, an old
Middlesex cricketer, was in practice as a doctor, he went up to
Oxford and got his Blue in his third year, 1913, largely on the
strength of an innings of 129 in an hour and a half against M.C.C.,
in which, *Wisden* says, he hit with delightful freedom all round the
wicket. In 1914 he had a poor season and lost his place. He had also
represented Oxford twice in the hurdles. In the war he was shot
through the right hand and narrowly avoided amputation. As it
was, though he could put his hand on the bat it had little strength.

His beautiful cutting, however, remained as much a feature of his play as his skill on the leg. Despite his handicap he was not a slow scorer. Almost as remarkable as his batting was his fielding. Though much of the work on his right side had to be done back-handed by his left hand, he was never reckoned a liability in the field.

For years he was a regular member of the Army side, which he often captained, and most of his other cricket was played for the Household Brigade, Eton Ramblers, I Zingari, Harlequins, Free Foresters and other clubs. As a member of A.C. MacLaren's side to Australia and New Zealand in 1922–23, he scored 689 runs with an average of 28.70, his highest score being 102 against Canterbury during which he added 282 with A.P.F. Chapman in two and a quarter hours. Even after the Second World War he continued to make runs in club cricket and he himself believed that the century which he made in his last innings was the 100th of his career. In any case it was a fitting finale to the career of a brave and determined man.

WILLIAMS, BENJAMIN HUNTSMAN, was killed in Rhodesia on August 3, 1978, when the vehicle in which he was travelling came under a rocket attack from terrorists. He is the first first-class cricketer to have lost his life in the present conflict. Huntsman Williams, a left-arm fast-medium bowler, won Rhodesian Nuffield and South African Schools' Caps in 1961 and 1962 and, while still a schoolboy, played for Rhodesian Country Districts against the visiting New Zealand team in 1961–62, taking four wickets for 89 in the first innings. He made his first-class debut in 1966–67 and was a regular member of the Rhodesian team in 1969–70 when he took four wickets for 56 against Transvaal in Salisbury, his best analysis. Thereafter he played no more. His total career covered eight first-class matches. Born in Bulawayo on June 10, 1944, he was 34.

WILSON, HERBERT G., born on January 9, 1864, died at Winnipeg on January 16, 1925. An effective bowler at his best, he took 39 wickets for 65 runs while on tour with the Winnipeg C.C. in 1887, and in 1895 played for Canada v. United States. He was a member of the Expedition for the relief of General Gordon at Khartoum in 1884 and also a Klondyke pioneer.

WINSER, LEGH, who died in Australia on December 20, 1983, aged 99, was at the time the oldest living Sheffield Shield cricketer. Born in Cheshire and educated at Oundle, he played for Staffordshire from 1906 to 1908, keeping wicket to S.F. Barnes, at the time perhaps the world's deadliest bowler. Emigrating to South Australia in 1909, Winser was soon keeping wicket for that state. By 1913 he had become a strong candidate for a place in the Australian team to South Africa, a tour that was, in fact, cancelled because of the onset of war.

After giving up cricket he achieved eminence as an amateur golfer, winning the Championship of South Australia eight times and the Australian Amateur Championship once. At the time of the Bodyline tour, in 1932–33, he was secretary to the Governor of South Australia, Sir Alexander Hore-Ruthven (afterwards the Earl of Gowrie). Hore-Ruthven being in England at the time, Winser was intimately concerned with the exchange of cables between the Australian Board of Control and M.C.C. when, after ugly scenes in the Adelaide Test match, the future of the tour, indeed of the special relationship between the United Kingdom and Australia, was put in jeopardy. In his later years, spent at Barwon Heads, near Geelong in Victoria, he regularly beat his age at golf, on one occasion by no fewer than 11 strokes: when 87 he played the 18 holes of the Barwon Heads links in 76 shots.

WODEHOUSE, SIR PELHAM GRENVILLE, the famous novelist who died in hospital on Long Island on February 14, 1975, at the age of 93, had been a member of the Dulwich College XI in 1899 and 1900. He was godfather of M.G. Griffith, the late captain of Sussex.

WOODROFFE, SIDNEY CLAYTON (8th Rifle Brigade), was killed at
Hooge on July 30, 1916, while showing such bravery that he was
awarded the VC. He was a brother of K.H.C. Woodroffe, and played
cricket at Marlborough, but was not in the XI. He was 19 years of age.

WOOSNAM, MAXWELL, who died on July 14, 1965, aged 72, was one of
the greatest all-round amateur sportsmen of his day. He captained
Winchester in 1911, his second season in the XI, at cricket and golf.
In 1911, when *Wisden* described him as one of the School players of
the year, he hit 144 and 33 not out for a Public Schools XI against
M.C.C. at Lord's. Going up to Cambridge, he did not get a Blue for
cricket, though he was 12th man in the 1912 match against Oxford,
but he represented the University at Association football – captaining the side in 1914 – lawn tennis and real tennis.

   An outstanding centre-half, 'Max' played football for the
Corinthians, with whom he was on tour in Brazil when the First
World War broke out. After Army service, he played for three years
for Manchester City, whom he captained, and in 1922 became one of
the few amateurs to gain an England cap in a full international
when he was chosen as captain against Wales. At lawn tennis, he
and R. Lycett won the doubles at Wimbledon in 1921 when he also
captained the British Davis Cup team in America. At Antwerp in
1920 he won an Olympic Gold Medal as partner to O.G.N.
Turnbull in the men's doubles and a silver medal in the mixed doubles. He later did much good work for the International Lawn
Tennis Club of Great Britain.

WORNHAM, JEFFREY RICHARD TRISTAN, was killed tackling a fire on
February 2, 2005, aged 28. Jeff Wornham and a fellow fireman were
trying to rescue a woman trapped by a blaze in a tower block in
Stevenage, Hertfordshire. All three died. Cricket was Wornham's
enduring love. As a boy, he spent much of the summer dressed in
whites on the off chance that he might find a game he could join. A

teacher, faced with a moderate academic record, explained Wornham's school year: spring term to prepare for cricket, summer term to play it and autumn term to relive the matches. He also played for Reed C.C., helping them to the Hertfordshire Colts Championship in 1990, and rejoining the club after college. He made useful runs with his correct, left-handed batting and kept wicket after a snowboarding accident hampered his bowling. 'Soul Limbo' – the signature tune for the BBC's cricket coverage – was played at his funeral, and his ashes scattered over the Lord's outfield. On the evening of the fire, he was knocking in his new bat, bought earlier that day.

WORSLEY, FRANCIS, died in a London hospital on September 15, 1949. He was best known as producer of the radio variety programme *ITMA*, but in his younger days he played cricket for Glamorgan during seasons 1922 and 1923, and always retained his love for the game. Worsley was educated at Brighton College and Oxford and formerly held a scholastic appointment.

WORTHINGTON, PRIMROSE, who died on January 23, 1999, aged 93, was the last surviving grandchild of W.G. Grace. She remembered sitting on his knee and tying ribbons in his beard.

WREFORD BROWN, CHARLES, the amateur footballer and soccer legislator who played first-class cricket between 1886 and 1889, died at his home in London on November 26, 1951, aged 85. A free hitter, a slow bowler with a break either way and a good field at mid-off, Wreford Brown captained Charterhouse, and in 1887 he would have been in the Oxford team against Cambridge but for an accident. He occasionally assisted Gloucestershire, the county of his birth, and he visited America with Lord Hawke's team in 1891.

As a soccer player, Wreford Brown achieved fame as a centre-half, although he could fill any position. He captained Oxford against Cambridge in 1889 and gained four caps for England, one when he led his team to notable victory against Scotland in Glasgow in 1898. He helped Old Carthusians and Corinthians. He became vice-president of the Football Association and for many years was chairman of the F.A. International Selection committee. He kept in trim even when undertaking legislative duties, and at 60 he turned out for Corinthians against Eton.

Wreford Brown, who was a solicitor, made many trips abroad with F.A. teams as member in charge, and a good tale is told of him in this connection. A fine chess player, his keenness for the game led him into an embarrassing situation during one visit to the colonies. On arrival he was greeted by an old friend, a high officer of the home Association, also an enthusiastic chess player. All tour matters forgotten for the moment, the pair slipped off to a little café for a game, and there they stayed for several hours oblivious of the fact that officials were searching in vain for them and that the lunch of welcome had to go on without them.